Life Reset

Life Reset

The Awareness Integration Path to Create the Life You Want

Foojan Zeine

ROWMAN & LITTLEFIELD
Lanham • Boulder • New York • London

Published by Rowman & Littlefield
A wholly owned subsidiary of The Rowman & Littlefield Publishing Group, Inc.
4501 Forbes Boulevard, Suite 200, Lanham, Maryland 20706
www.rowman.com

Unit A, Whitacre Mews, 26-34 Stannary Street, London SE11 4AB

British Library Cataloguing in Publication Information Available

Library of Congress Cataloging-in-Publication Data

978-1-4422-7609-3 (cloth)
978-1-4422-7610-9 (electronic)

♾️™ The paper used in this publication meets the minimum requirements of
American National Standard for Information Sciences—Permanence of Paper
for Printed Library Materials, ANSI/NISO Z39.48-1992.

Printed in the United States of America

Contents

Acknowledgments

The journey to the creation of the Awareness Integration (AI) Model has been a long, yet amazing, experience. I'd like to thank the pioneers in the field of psychology and ontology for bringing a wealth of information into this field, allowing me to use their brilliant work as components of the model. Many thanks to Nasrin Barkhordari, Ladan Safvati, Sholeh Warner, Fazi Azimi, Melina Satari, Julian Farzan, Lilian Farzan, Jake Gavenas, Sanam Rahimzadeh, Sara Panhasi, Shadi Kohandarvish, Shayan Rad, and Amy Firestein for their support in conducting and organizing research and publishing of the AI Model. Dr. Fereshteh Mirhashemi, Lili Starr and Helen Gilhooly, I thank you for creating the space of empowerment and love so that I felt the strength to pursue my dream of creating a model based on what I had learned and integrated in my life and my career. I'm so grateful to have Eileen Manoukian in my life with her resourcefulness and caring. Thank you Kevin Quirk for the art of listening and making what I meant into the great art of writing. Thank you Lenore Skomal for taking this book under your wings and carrying it through; I call you the guardian angel. And finally, and most importantly, I'm blessed to have Sam as my mate and for allowing me to experience love as I have never felt before.

Author's Note

The information contained in this book is intended to provide helpful and informative material. The ideas, procedures, and suggestions are not intended to serve as a replacement for professional advice, psychotherapy, or the provision of psychological services. Any use of this information is at the reader's discretion. All matters regarding your health require medical supervision. Neither the author nor the publisher shall be liable or responsible for any loss or damage allegedly arising from any information or suggestion in this book.

Introduction

You picked up this book for a reason. You're ready to hit the Life Reset button.

Clearly, you're feeling unfulfilled in your life. Despite your best efforts and intentions, maybe you're not getting what you really want and need in your work, your intimate relationships, or in your dealings with family, friends, and even strangers.

At times you may feel weighed down by voices that proclaim, "I'm not good enough" or, "I just don't seem to fit." Or you may wake up feeling powerless, angry, or frustrated about people or situations you have to face every day. Maybe you've been let down by others so many times that you wonder who you can really trust. Maybe you yearn for greater connection with the world around you but feel afraid of becoming bigger than you've allowed yourself to be. Perhaps you've achieved a degree of success but somehow you're still not completely happy. Or you're aware that childhood wounds still burden or limit you, and although you've done your best to move past them, you still get angry, frustrated, or just plain stuck.

You deserve to be happy, to have what you want, and to obtain the freedom to be who you really are as you find your place in the world. You'll feel stronger and more capable of asserting yourself, and your thoughts, feelings, and behavior will be in greater alignment. Realistically, you still won't be able to change what has happened to you in the past. But you'll learn that with greater freedom in your mind and more love in you heart you can choose to deal with those same situations in healthier, more productive ways, exercising greater responsibility and accountability in how you relate to yourself and others.

I'm confident that no matter why you have turned to this book, if you commit yourself fully and wholeheartedly to the process that unfolds, you'll take a very big step toward greater fulfillment.

As you read this book you'll soon be addressing your life through a much wider lens, and trust me, it won't be scary. Instead of worrying, get psyched because it'll be fun. This journey is designed to help you free yourself from all those negative thoughts and experiences that have heretofore defined you, and it is going to be one of the most fascinating of your life. And I'll be with you every step of the way. I'm going to escort you on a unique life journey—a fascinating and revealing path. On this path you'll be examining seven major areas of your life with many subareas. You'll meet a great number of people, both familiar and unfamiliar. It's a bit like putting together your autobiography.

I'm going to ask you a series of simple questions, and through your answers you'll be exploring your thoughts, feelings, and behaviors. What you discover may at various times surprise, challenge, and excite you as you expand and deepen your awareness of who you are and why you do what you do. Sometimes I'll invite you to name an emotion you are experiencing and then guide you through a simple process to be present with and release that emotion. That release will help clear space to bring in more of what you want in life.

Once you have visited each of these areas of life, I'll walk you back along the same path. As you revisit each of the seven areas of life, you'll be thrilled with the change. You'll hold new beliefs, new values, and even new intentions about how to relate to the people and situations in your "real" life. With this fresh perspective, a changed identity can be directed toward more satisfying results; and you'll have new goals supported by concrete action plans to achieve them. You will have successfully hit the Life Reset button.

This new therapeutic Life Reset process has a name: the Awareness Integration Model. I've been utilizing concepts from this process for many years, but I formally launched the technique in 2012. Since then I've introduced it to hundreds of health-care professionals and clients from all walks of life.

I've witnessed the results in the many clients I've guided along this same path. I've been a psychotherapist since 1990, and I can honestly say that I had never witnessed clients consistently walk out the door of my office looking like completely different human beings, after only a matter of weeks of therapeutic work, until I began utilizing this therapeutic model. When I conducted a pilot study of clients who had completed this process, the results showed a marked decrease in depression and anxiety and a significant increase in self-esteem. I don't know that I've suddenly become a better therapist; I've simply found a more effective way to facilitate profound growth, change, and healing.

Awareness Integration is designed to enhance self-awareness, increase self-esteem, release past traumas or psychological blocks, reduce the symptoms of anxiety and depression, and promote a clear, realistic, and positive attitude to learn and implement new skills for an effective, productive, and successful life. The model integrates cognitive, behavioral, emotional, and body-mind techniques to create more awareness into a person's life patterns of thinking, feeling, and behaving toward self and others.

Through this model you begin to see the correlation between how you perceive the world, make decisions about yourself based on your identity, relate and act toward the world as that identity, and create results toward supporting that decided-upon self-identity.

I came upon this new approach after more than three decades of learning and practicing dozens of therapeutic methods and techniques, both personally and professionally. I became thoroughly familiar with the benefits of cognitive-behavioral, emotional, existential, and body-mind theories. I learned and practiced such techniques as inner-child work, hypnosis, Eye Movement Desensitization and Reprocessing (EMDR), and the Sedona Method for identifying and releasing emotions. I also trained and practiced in the emerging field of ontology via the Bonyan method and landmark education. Everything was useful in some contexts. And yet I still noted that my clients would often get stuck.

Something was missing—an approach that would integrate the best of these diverse therapeutic methods into one dynamic, easy-to-practice model that would steer clients toward profound, tangible change and growth. I also wanted a method structured enough so that anyone could follow and execute it and yet be flexible enough so that individual therapists could also tailor it to their strengths.

That's how the Awareness Integration Model was born. It's been gratifying to witness its growth and success with my own clients and in the work of professional therapists whom I have trained in the method. Yet I will be the first to admit that this model isn't totally new. I've taken what I've learned from other teachings and teachers and done my best to bring it all together with a new structure and specific components designed to get at the root of what holds us back. Hopefully by utilizing pieces from many effective interventions I have created a pathway that allows people of all ages and backgrounds to see the whole picture of their lives and, from that view, to facilitate profound, lasting change.

I invite you to step fully into this process and discover for yourself where it may take you. My role is simply to frame the questions and offer you guiding tips on how you might respond to them as well as to offer insights and examples from my work with others like you. You'll be having your own experience. You're in charge!

So let's dive into a further understanding of how this new model works and then step firmly and boldly onto the path that lies ahead.

Chapter One

Awareness Awakened

How the Model Works

One of the major differences between human beings and animals is that we have the capacity to be self-aware. We have the ability to watch ourselves—what we think, what we feel, and how we behave. And we're able to self-reflect by asking ourselves questions: Why did I do that? How did it impact me and others around me? What can I learn from this experience? And if we take it a step further we can ask ourselves, "What thoughts, feelings, or experiences from my past has affected what I do in my day-to-day life. How can I begin to let go of them so I can bring my life into alignment with my best intentions?"

Yes, we have a great capacity to be self-aware. And self-awareness can be a very effective and dynamic tool. Nathaniel Branden asserts, "Living consciously [with self-awareness] is a source of power and liberation. It does not weigh us down—it lifts us up."[1]

Yet we're not fully tapping that power. Most of the time, we do not use and practice self-awareness with a firm commitment to utilize it to its optimum. We just don't fully embrace it. The one ability we have as a species that animals lack, we barely acknowledge.

So what are we missing out on when we don't learn and practice true self-awareness? It's not just understanding ourselves better, though that is the critical first step. The real benefit comes from taking what we see and learn through practicing self-awareness and using it to make healthier, more productive choices in our lives. It's that possibility of imagining ourselves in the future and working toward a more dynamic image or vision. As physicist Michio Kaku explains, "Self-awareness is creating a model of the world and simulating the future in which you appear."[2]

The Awareness Integration Model creates an opportunity for you to become the master of self-awareness, making you more responsible and more accountable for who you are in your thoughts, emotions, and behavior. Just

1

as important, self-awareness provides you with a greater capacity to move through past psychological traumas and blocks, which creates much more space for you to integrate desired changes.

When I was assisting clients as a motivational coach or when I focused on brief cognitive therapy in working with clients as a therapist, I would often notice something fascinating about the practice of teaching people new skills. They usually loved learning the skill and would eagerly set out to practice it in their life. Then something would happen to sabotage them, leaving them to ask, "What happened? Why wasn't I able to tap into that new skill?" What happened was that they were not aware of the blocks or traumas from the past that were buried inside them, just waiting to catch them in their best attempt to try out a new behavior. Some part of them that needed attention was not going to let the change happen.

That's why the lens of self-awareness is so important. It promotes clarity and a positive attitude—shining the light and clearing out the path to follow toward new behavior.

When you've learned new skills to apply in your life within the process of following the model, the probability of succeeding at those new skills is much higher because you employ self-awareness. You're better positioned to sustain the desired results. Those sabotaging blocks or traumas that kept standing in your way of mastering new relationship skills, new skills to lose weight, or new skills to conquer a negative habit will now be pushed to the side of the road. You'll be free to march forward and build a more effective and productive life.

Bringing self-awareness to your thoughts, feelings, and behavior allows you to be more responsible for what you do not only in your own life but also with life all around you. Taking a more responsible approach, you may say, "No matter what else happens in my life, I choose to be happy." Or you may choose to be generous, loving, or patient. Those are the kinds of choices you can make and then act on consciously regardless of circumstances. You might say, "I choose to be happy," and then get into an accident. This would naturally put a damper on your happiness. However, if you are truly committed to pursuing the intention you stated and to have it as a conscious reality in your life, you can attend to the accident; handle all the natural feelings that arise, such as fear, anger, sadness, and so forth; and shift yourself back to happiness. Self-awareness is the key to facilitating the path toward this shift.

For example, let's say you reacted to painful experiences from your past by adopting a belief that the world is bad and not to be trusted. By clinging to that negative belief, you only see the distrust and the bad behavior in the world. You don't see the love and generosity. Even if you tell yourself that you're going to trust people more, if you haven't released the trauma associated with your belief that the world is bad, you're not going to succeed. You may trust for two minutes, but something bad may happen and then you'll just go back to how you've always been. Through self-awareness, however, you understand that you're the one creating this belief that the world is bad. It's not the world that is unworthy of your trust; it is you creating this belief as a general concept. Then, when you shed light on the past hurt that triggered this belief and consciously release it, you open the door to a self-aware choice. You can confidently proclaim, "I'm going to be more trusting, no matter how people around me act," and you now have the awareness to live ever closer to that reality.

Perhaps your heightened self-awareness will lead you to vow that you're not going to live in fear. Again, your intention doesn't mean that fear won't ever come up in your life. Rather, you'll no longer be ruled or guided by your fear. Or you may choose a different way to be in your marriage. You establish the intention that you are going to be a more caring partner and you strive to uphold that intention, even during inevitable periods of strain.

These choices that emerge from a positive attitude and the creation of a new reality that you'll gain while following the Awareness Integration journey are more powerful and more effective than simple affirmations. An affirmation without the self-awareness to look at your behavior and bring out the blocks that keep you from changing it often remains just a fantasy.

Once you gain greater self-awareness and you work with the blocks that hold you back from being who you want to be, you'll just naturally start making healthier choices. I've never come across anyone who would choose negative intentions or destructive values when given the freedom to access greater choice.

Clients who have worked with the Awareness Integration Model consistently move toward a value system that promotes respect, kindness, love, and personal integrity. Then, by continuing to practice their enhanced self-awareness skills, they can consistently look at their behavior and compare it to their intentionality, asking themselves, "Am I doing what I say I want to do? Am I creating what I want to create?"

You'll discover just how important a deepening sense of self-awareness is in your quest to make meaningful and lasting change in your life. The questions that you'll be responding to are designed to facilitate that self-awareness, which will steer you toward the kind of enhanced consciousness we have been discussing. Becoming more self-aware will enable you to claim a sense of ownership, responsibility, and accountability regarding the creation of your thoughts, emotions, behavior, and results.

Along the way you'll have many opportunities to bring forth the origins of your past decision making about yourself and the world and then heal the precipitating experiences of those events that led to negative core beliefs you've held. When we identify and address these negative core beliefs and release the stored emotions that created them, real healing occurs. Then, as the healed part of us integrates with all the other parts of us, we will be much better equipped to choose more positive beliefs, values, and intentions.

Self-awareness and integration, then, combine to form a vital part of the foundation of this model. When you embark on the Awareness Integration journey, you'll be uncovering what you think, feel, and do in every realm of life. As part of your experience, you'll have profound moments of retrieving what is in your subconscious and bringing it into consciousness. That's often where the real "action" takes place—opening the door to the change you deeply long for. So often I see and hear people passionately speak about what they do not want in their lives, when a close examination of their actions reveals that they have been busy creating exactly what it is they don't want.

JUDY'S STORY

When I worked with my client Judy on losing her unwanted weight, although we spent many weeks organizing and structuring how, what, and when she would eat and exercise, every morning her unmotivated and angry mood took over and she found some justifiable reason not to follow what she had committed to. In working through the negative core belief that she had created when she was eight years old when a classmate called her "ugly monkey" even though she had worn her best new dress to school, she decided then and there that *I am ugly no matter what I do.* Against all the evidence that she is beautiful, since she is a print fashion model, Judy, even at age forty-five, wakes up every morning thinking that no matter what she does she will remain ugly.

This thought with all the emotions attached to it haunts her and takes her away from her commitment and the skills that she has to create the result of reaching and keeping her ideal weight and figure. Through the Awareness Integration Model she was able to connect with the eight-year-old part of her who was still separate from her adulthood and all other experience that she had as a beautiful woman. Through this connection she was able to release the emotions and then the beliefs that were created by the eight-year-old she was; thus she was able to heal that part and integrate it into the whole system. Judy was able go from the belief that *I am ugly no matter what* to *I can make myself beautiful no matter what.* This new belief created a motivation and commitment to keep the structure that was created for her to lose weight, and she lost twenty-five pounds and has kept it off.

Through the comprehensive approach of Awareness Integration, you'll be far better positioned to align your desires with your day-to-day experience.

As I developed the Awareness Integration Model, I came to see that the foundation of the approach could be described through the lens of nine basic principles.

1. Reality is the experience of the observer/perceiver. Every human being observes/perceives and creates reality based on his or her state of being, beliefs, emotions, and behaviors. Human beings are co-creators of reality.

   Our personal reality is as much a product of emotion as it is of thought and rationality. Our experience will always be a subjective reality. We usually create our own version of reality based on distinctions of pleasure versus pain or comfort versus discomfort and then make up complex formulas around our reality. When we insist that our subjective reality is the one and only reality, we more easily get into fights and power struggles trying to defend it. We don't see that this reality we cling to is just how we perceive a situation; it's not absolute. We need to look at our personal reality to discover how it got in our head, as we also ask ourselves the key question: Is this reality actually serving me in my life?

2. Every human being has the capability and potential to learn the skills to have an enjoyable, functional, and successful life.

   The brain is a living system that is open and dynamic, which means it is forever in a state of change, according to neuropsychiatrist Daniel Siegel,[3] who has written many books about how our brain functions. It can continue to emerge and reshape itself with the changing environment and the changing state of its own activity.

3. These skills are learned through physical and psychological development, one's own experiences, and mirroring parents, teachers, peers, media, and culture.

   We learn our skills from our surroundings and then turn them into subconscious patterns of living. In that way, we live on automatic pilot from generation to generation. For example, if we grew up in a family system where yelling and screaming was the norm and saw that behavior as a powerful tool to get the result that we want, there's a pretty good chance we have found ourselves in adult living situations where much of the communication was conducted through yelling and screaming.

   However, if we felt powerless in that surrounding and experienced it more as a painful and anxiety-producing environment, we avoided it at all cost and tried to create conflict-free interactions. Each of those decisions, whether it is an attachment to a certain behavior or an aversion toward a behavior, limits our way of being. Yet so often we don't even know where we picked up these patterns; they are simply what we know as a natural way of being and behaving since they are all around us and appear to be the norm.

4. The human mind perceives and creates meaning internally for all external stimuli that results in a subjective reality that may vary from actual events and realities of others. Through the invented reality, one creates formulas, beliefs, and personal identities that relate to self, others, and the universe at large.

   In other words, out of all the experiences that we acquire from the world around us as a child we create assumptions and beliefs about the world and ourselves. Over time, those assumptions and beliefs get reinforced by similar experiences and turn into automatic thought patterns. Henry Stapp explains, "A person tends to experience what he or she is looking for, provided the potentiality for that experience is present."[4] In that way, our subjective awareness is not challenged. We simply develop a set of formulas and rules consciously at one point in life to create certain identities to survive life at its best and then live based on those sets of rules that were created at a very young age every day, subconsciously. We create one way of being and behaving at home with our parents or siblings and other ways of being with our extended family, teachers at school, friends, lovers, bosses, employees and coworkers, or society at large.

5. Human beings store experiences cognitively, emotionally, and somatically. The unintegrated experiences await integration. Negative core beliefs, including the emotions that are produced by them and the area of the body experiencing the emotions at the time of the original incident, repeatedly resurface in automatic thinking patterns. These negative core beliefs create a withholding and survival-based attitude. This attitude is triggered by an event, creates a result that prohibits the individual from achieving, and holds back one's ability to live a fulfilled life.

   When one experiences an event that produces a negative emotion or is traumatizing and one does not handle, feel, and release (the process of release is shown to them in the intervention) the produced emotion appropriately, a certain generalized negative belief about self or others gets created as a protective measure to survive the similar negative experiences that emerge in the future. The negative core beliefs created by the trauma become fixated with their own set of emotions, sensations, and behaviors that reinforce them.

   As a result, we approach much of life with an automatic, outdated, or unworkable attitude. So if we don't uncover and transform these negative core beliefs, we are prone to living in a constant state of surviving. We are simply not flourishing. We may be held back in our work, in our relationships, or in any realm of life. Things may be going along just fine and then, boom! Someone says or does something that triggers a childhood memory, and we immediately tumble back into our negative, crippling core belief.

6. As the unintegrated belief-emotion-body state is attended to, released, and integrated into the whole system, neutral and positive attitudes, beliefs, and emotions can be experienced.

When we suffer a painful experience in childhood, we often get over-whelmed. In response, we shut down our emotions and turn to survival skills just to persevere. That's often a necessary and healthy response when we are children, and yet those emotions that we were unable to handle back then cry out for our attention today. As adults with enhanced self-awareness, we have the opportunity and the skills to go back and look at those painful emotions from the lens of who we are today. When we do that and we release the stored and un-dealt-with emotions that have been blocking our way, we shine a light on the path that leads to the creation of a new way of being.

MARY'S STORY

Mary at age four hid behind the couch when her father yelled at her mother; she thought that her father was so dangerous that her mother would leave. Her little body shook while she held herself. She felt fear all over her body. She could smell her father's sweat and the ring of his voice in her ear. She thought that she had to survive the yelling and then run to her mom to prevent her from leaving her. Mary decided that she was powerless against anger and that, when anger happens, she will be abandoned.This thought with all the emotions attached to it haunts her and takes her away from her commitment and the skills that she has to create the result of reaching and keeping her ideal weight and figure.

The accumulation of negative core beliefs such as these becomes the foundation of our identity in many different areas of our life, limiting us in how we react to all kinds of situations. Mary at age forty on a date with a forty-five-year-old saw her date get angry at the waiter, and her anxiety rose; her body started shaking so much that she had to hold herself, and she even started smelling her father's sweat. She told her date that she had to go home and did not want to finish her dinner. That's the script waiting to be rewritten when we bring in Awareness Integration. Mary was able to heal and change the earlier belief that she was powerless against anger and to see her strength and how she did use her power when she asked to end the dinner. She replaced her belief to *I am able to take control of myself in the face of others' anger*, which helped her feel powerful and in control.

7. Through self-awareness, integration of one's experiences, and the creation of conscious choices regarding beliefs, emotions, and actions, one can choose a positive attitude for the creation of a new, positive reality and therefore produce intended results.

As we complete with the unfinished emotional baggage from the past and integrate all of our unattended emotional parts, we have more accessibility to our subconscious needs, desires, and wants. Now we can make more conscious choices about the way we choose to think, feel, and behave toward people and matters in front of us versus reacting to it from an old, unworkable, and outdated belief. When healing takes place, inevitably we choose a healthy and positive attitude toward growth. From this new conscious, healthy, and positive attitude we can create a vision about the future and set goals and choose behaviors that lead us to create the results we intend.

8. New skills can be learned and practiced in a neutral and positive environment to enhance life's capabilities, experiences, results, and relationships. Research shows that children learn new information and skills much more effectively in a calm and positive environment, which are therefore applied and sustained through life.

9. Conscious intentionality and envisioning of a desired result, in combination with effective planning and timely scheduled action plans, raise the probability of achieving the desired results in all areas of life. This is where fantasy becomes tangible reality. Ideas are abstract and in our imagination; only when the idea is put into a schedule with tangible action is the desired result created.

WHAT MAKES AWARENESS INTEGRATION UNIQUE

Whether you are a trained professional or someone who is preparing to experience the Awareness Integration Model to apply it to your own life, you may recognize that these nine principles freely borrow from and integrate many established, effective therapeutic models and techniques. My goal in developing this process has been to bring together those many influences in a dynamic and effective way—to provide the greatest opportunity for comprehensive, lasting change in our work, our relationships, our way of dealing with money, and our manner of relating to the world around us.

The journey form of the model and the open-ended questions provide a new structure and context for exploring your life patterns and where they come from. The focus on harmonizing your thoughts, feelings, and behavior provides the foundation for relating to every aspect of your life in a more positive way. Building a new intended reality, backed by life-affirming values and the establishment of concrete goals and the skills required to achieve them, takes what may at times seem to be a familiar therapeutic process and moves it toward a new and exciting end. You really do create the opportunity to hit your Life Reset button!

Another significant way that Awareness Integration takes the principles of other techniques and shifts them to new ground emerges through the process of releasing stored emotions linked to negative core beliefs that have had a limiting and destructive influence on our lives for years. Many other therapeutic models help to facilitate emotional release, but the added dimension with Awareness Integration is in going back to an impactful memory through three different doorways: (1) the emotion itself, (2) the location in the body where that emotion is stored, and (3) the core belief attached to that memory. This approach taps into the neural network pathways, where a true release of stored emotions and their crippling effect has the best chance of occurring. Too often in my experience, I have seen emotional work that encourages a catharsis, but nothing in that person's life actually changes as the result of all that crying. And real change is what we're after!

Shaping the model as a journey fits because it provides anyone who follows the Awareness Integration journey with ample opportunities to pinpoint key beliefs and issues across a wide spectrum of their life, and then look at them from many different perspectives. You'll soon discover for yourself how that works. As I mentioned in the introduction, you may at times be surprised by the discoveries you make regarding what you really think and feel about life around you and how experiences from your past are limiting you in the present. As you proceed along this journey, things will just keep popping up. And they're all there to serve you in your quest for a more satisfying life.

Here's a preview of those seven areas of life that you'll be visiting in the chapters ahead as you follow the Awareness Integration journey:

From Strangers to Friends: Taking a look at how you generally feel about people you don't know, acquaintances, extended family members, and friends.

Career and Money: Examining your attitude and relationship to jobs and career, authority/bosses/employees, and money-earning-/-spending patterns.

Just a Bit Closer: Looking at your relationship to your siblings, significant people in your life, and in-laws.

Love and Romance (and All the By-products): Focusing on your intimate/romantic relationships, sexuality, and the relationship with your children.

Mom and Dad: Exploring your relationship with your mom and dad as you were growing up right up until now. You'll also be looking at their relationship to each other and how it affected you.

Me and Me: Your relationship with your body, love, addiction, illnesses, and
  finally, you and your identity.
Beyond the "I": How you interact and view nature, the universe, god/spiritu-
  ality, and death.

As you glance over this list, you'll get an idea of how comprehensive your
journey ahead will be. With so many diverse realms of life to visit, you can
be confident that you're going to learn a lot about yourself and how you look
at and relate to life. You're also going to feel many emotions, some intensely
perhaps, and others more subtly. All of your feelings and insights will be
valuable. The journey will also provide ample opportunities to begin making
significant changes in your life. I trust that you'll experience moments of real
excitement about what lies ahead.

As a reminder, after you have completed the process of spending time in
each of the seven areas of life, you'll be going back to those same areas, stopping for shorter visits. On that return journey, you'll be carrying new values and
intentions, guiding you toward changed ways of looking at and being in your
life. This is often the most energizing and life-transforming part of the Awareness Integration journey. Imagine going back to each of those life areas and
groups of people and asking, Who am I in this area now? What is the identity I
intend to bring with me here? Perhaps you'll proclaim, "I am a capable, powerful person." So how will you now behave toward your career? What new skills
will you need to practice? The possibilities for change truly open up.

Rest assured that you'll be moving through these seven life areas in a
gradual progression at your own pace. Some areas will be more engaging and
revealing for you than others. You can spend as much as time as you need
with any particular area. This is your own unique experience. Some areas of
life may not apply to you at all. If you're not married, you may choose not to
stop at the in-laws area of life. If you don't have children, you might bypass
that area. However, as you'll see when you reach such life areas, there may
be good reason for you to explore that realm even if it does not at first seem
to fit.

Don't be concerned if you feel initially unclear about what any one particular area will encompass. For example, you may already be scratching your
head trying to imagine what it means to "be with death." Each area of life will
be clearly described as we come to it on the journey.

PREPPING FOR THE AWARENESS INTEGRATION JOURNEY

You'll need to choose the method you'll use to track your responses to the
questions. You may feel comfortable writing your responses in a journal, per-

haps one specifically chosen for doing the Awareness Integration Model and adorned in a way that fits your purpose and intention for taking the journey. You may instead choose to type your answers on your laptop. If you don't feel comfortable with writing, you may turn to your favorite audio-recording device and speak your answers. When I initially developed this model, I took it myself before introducing it to any of my clients. I wrote my answers, but in the process I noticed that I tend to sound more positive in my journaling and more dramatic when I speak out loud. If you get more juice from either writing or talking that may determine which way you go in following the process. You also may decide to set up a video system so you can both see and hear yourself responding to the questions.

Perhaps you'll need to experiment in the early stages to find the right fit. The idea is to choose a way of responding that feels comfortable and that will allow you to focus your attention on the process of sinking into the questions. If you do select the writing method, give yourself full permission to use different colors, or to capitalize, circle, and underline words or phrases for emphasis—especially when you are giving voice to your emotions. Similarly, if you're typing on your laptop you may want to change color or font size as well as bring in boldface, italics, or all caps to highlight something important.

Whether you are writing or orally speaking your responses, consider supplementing your words with drawings, pictures, or other visual representations. Such creative expressions can help you more strongly identify with something that you revealed or discovered during one of your visits to an area of life. And give yourself freedom to get in your angry voice when that's called for, or go on the Internet and find an image that perfectly conveys what you mean or what you feel and paste it in your journal.

Because you are doing this process alone, you may want to consider sharing your answers with someone else. Perhaps you have a confidante, someone you feel safe and comfortable with, who knows you well, whose opinion you respect, and who won't judge you or leave you feeling as if you're talking to a blank wall. If you are currently working with a therapist, you may find great benefit in bringing in your work from doing this model to complement your therapeutic process. For some people who embark on the Awareness Integration journey, sharing what they come up with can be a powerful way to add depth to their responses. For others, it may feel essential to keep all their answers private. You'll know what's best for you.

It's also very important to recognize when you may need the help of a therapist. Whether or not you are currently seeing a psychotherapist, the need to consult a trained professional may emerge when you are diving into emotional realms and seeking to release old traumas. This model is designed to help you feel comfortable in exploring your feelings and to have the experience of safely releasing intense emotions associated with memories from your past while working on your own. But if the emotional "charge" does not go away or intensifies after doing a particular exercise, you may need to call upon a therapist's guidance. Therapists are experts whose eyes and ears are trained for therapeutic listening, and they have the skills and techniques to help you continue your emotional work so you can heal from a trauma and move on, rather than being stuck in it.

I encourage you to complete the entire Awareness Integration journey, visiting all seven areas of life and then going back to those areas with a changed identity and new values on your return journey. This process is designed in such a way that the full benefits are more likely to emerge if you follow it completely. However, if you have reached a point in the journey where your intuition strongly informs you that you have gained just what you needed to find, putting aside the model is a choice you are free to make. You can always come back to it later. You really are in charge.

BETWEEN SESSIONS, THE AWARENESS CONTINUES

How should you schedule your sessions in working with each area of life on the Awareness Integration journey? There is no right or wrong approach. At the outset, you may want to set aside an hour or so each week to cover one area and then adjust as you need or want to. Or you may want to begin at a slower or a quicker pace. It's up to you.

It's best to work with Awareness Integration in a quiet, private space. If you have kids around, you may want to go to a park or some other environment where you won't be interrupted. If you do lose focus from time to time, the act of writing or speaking your responses will serve to bring you to full attention.

No matter how you schedule your sessions on your Awareness Integration journey, I want to emphasize one very important point: Your work will go on between sessions. Yes, the observation of how you think, feel, and behave in each area of real life as you deal with people is the most important part of the awareness and the integration toward your whole self. This also gives you the opportunity to do a reality check about your assumptions of how others think and feel about you.

These exercises will make you better equipped to notice what is happening in your life, to make more sense of it, and to devise new goals and strategies for you to make healthy changes.

Are you ready to reset your life? Here we go!

Chapter Two

From Strangers to Friends

You are about to start walking along a path, and on this path you are going to meet many different people in various area of your life. I will be asking you simple questions regarding your thoughts, feelings, and behavior as it relates to the people you encounter at each area. There are no right or wrong answers. You will notice many dualities within you. You simply capture what comes up for you in the moment. That is the art of self-awareness.

I also will ask you to identify feelings related to your answers. Then I will help you explore those emotions and the memories and beliefs associated with them. Again, there is no right or wrong way to have your experience.

To prepare for the start of the journey, go to the private, quiet place that you have chosen. Take out your journal, notebook, laptop, recorder, or any other tool that you've chosen to use. I recommend that you set aside forty-five to sixty minutes for this first area you will explore.

Ready?

The first group of people you are going to meet are people in the world—some seven and a half billion of them and counting. These are people from places near and far. You see them around when you drive your car, when you go to your grocery store, when you stop at your local Starbucks, or when you attend movies, plays, or concerts. You don't know these people personally, but they are there. Whether you recognize it or not, these people in the world that you don't know affect your life. Whenever you turn on the water, flick on your light switch, or push the button on your TV remote, there are contributions from countless people that helped make that act possible.

Now shift your attention from strangers out there in the world to your circle of acquaintances and extended family. These are people you know, some better than others, and some you can even consider as close or best friends. The people you will visit here may be women and men from your social network, parents of other children around the same age as yours, or those you know from a religious community or an organization you belong to.

As you widen your lens, consider extended family members that you see from time to time: aunts and uncles, cousins, nieces and nephews, and so forth. In terms of your acquaintances, you certainly may include your Facebook friends and contacts on other social media.

As you respond to the Awareness Integration journey questions in this area, you may notice differences between how you relate to those of the same gender and how your relate to those of the opposite gender. Your awareness may shed light on how social or antisocial you tend to be, or whether it's more difficult to break away from a connection with an extended family member versus an acquaintance.

Issues that have an emotional component in this life area may include a sense of being judged or rejected. I have worked with clients who became depressed simply because they didn't attract as many friend requests on Facebook as others. Another client revealed a sense of feeling controlled by her acquaintances, which brought up feelings of sadness and anger.

As you explore the questions ahead, one dynamic to keep in mind is how you may act in such a way to try to protect your reputation or popularity. We all have a critical need—almost an animal instinct—to feel we are part of the herd. Feeling pressured to be accepted to avoid losing our place in the herd, we may not reveal who we really are and what we really feel.

We project and maintain an image, which is a strategy that may backfire at times if it creates mistrust due to us portraying ourselves as not "real."

Even if we are not rejected by our acquaintances, our feelings may be triggered around them in a way that causes us pain. Now it's time to also zoom the camera in on your relationship with your close friends, including your best friend. These are the people that you trust to share who you really are, the ones who will be there for you regardless of what you are going through. They have passed the test of time to earn your trust. You know that you can say things to them that you might not share with anyone else, including your spouse, and they will hold it as sacred with no judgments.

Do you have such friends, or at least one best friend? You're going to take a closer look at those relationships now. Before turning to the questions of the model, it may be helpful to consider what determined how they became close friends. What were the criteria you used to let them in, and how did they "graduate" from being an acquaintance to a close friend? How did they choose to enter a close friendship with you? As an adult, is this process different from how you brought close friends into your life in childhood? For most of us, our childhood friendships were focused mostly on play, whereas close friendships as an adult tend to be linked to how we relate as people. Sometimes I hear people lament, "I can never re-create the close friendships

I had when I was young." Maybe that's because you can't be quite as trusting now as you were then because there seems to be more at stake. Conversely, other people say their friendships are more mature, more precious to them now. Think about what is true for you.

Friendships tend to look different depending on our gender. Men often choose close friends based on a shared activity or interest, such as sports, while women may look to their friends to lament about daily life experiences, or brainstorm how to handle a difficult situation. Your experience may fall within those general descriptions or transcend gender lines. Speaking of gender, do you have friends of the opposite gender? What do you look for and receive in those connections? Does attraction sometimes enter into the equation? If so, how do you handle that?

It's useful to examine our friendships and our feelings about them because friendship makes us vulnerable. Our feelings get involved, and childhood issues and trauma can show up. You will be experiencing how that is the case for you in a moment.

You can approach the questions in this life area in a couple of different ways. If you have one best friend, you can run through the full set of questions as it relates solely to that friendship. Then you can walk through the questions a second time, with an eye toward assessing your close friendships as a whole, with several people potentially involved. I recommend this dual approach.

When focusing on your group of close friends, you may want to add in your relationships with those who had been close friends at one time but no longer have that place in your life. What happened to change things? Did your friend cut off from you or vice versa? How did you feel about that loss?

JOHN'S STORY

John had a tendency to become aggressive when angry. Around his family, he was able to show those feelings with words or facial expressions and he was still accepted, but he feared being ostracized for behaving in that manner around acquaintances that didn't know him as well. So he put a lid on his aggressiveness. He became a real sweetheart, smiling and gracefully going along with things he really didn't believe in. Through his work in this area of the Awareness Integration journey, he recognized the split that had emerged in his behavior—putting on his smiley face while at the same time feeling angry toward others—and he was able to make healthy changes. Now he's acting more consistently, feeling free to refrain from doing something he doesn't believe in rather than caving to needless worry about looking too aggressive.

It's important to keep in mind that people often become our close friends due to some similarity in who we are and how we approach life. But who we are and how we live changes over the years, which sometimes precipitates a change in our friendships. Take an inventory of friends lost, and tune into your feelings about what was natural about that and where and when it may have left a scar.

Of course, you may find that you have mostly positive relationships with people, your acquaintances, extended family, and friends. You can simply appreciate how these connections enrich your life. Who knows what discoveries await you at this stop? Let's find out.

1. What do you think of people in the world, acquaintances, extended family, and friends?

   Ponder, reflect, and write about each group separately. Write both positive and negative thoughts. Do you like them, not like them, or have no opinion about them? Do you see them as good or not to be trusted? Do you regard them as kind and caring or selfish and manipulative? Or are you simply neutral toward them? Do you have an opinion about women that is different from how you look at men? Start writing or speaking what comes to mind. Your responses will simply reflect your attitudes and beliefs. They may sound familiar to you, or they may surprise you. Notice your dualities in the same areas or among different groups.

   As you reflect on these thoughts, you may want to consider how they have been shaped or influenced by what you learned from your own family or others when you were growing up. Perhaps you heard and adopted a belief such as "people can't be trusted, so you better watch out," "blacks are this; Muslims are that," or "people are greedy and out to get you." If you identify a belief that doesn't seem to have come from you, you can shine the light of awareness on it by asking yourself, Is this what I really believe? Does this attitude help me achieve my goals and live a happy life? If the answers come back "no," then you can choose to challenge those beliefs. It's also perfectly okay to accept your thoughts and beliefs as they are, especially if they are not something that drives your life.

   Do you really like having these people in your life, or have you just cultivated friendships out of need, without a high regard for many of these individuals? If your first response is to say, "It depends," explain what you mean: Do you feel uncomfortable around some friends and acquaintances but at ease around others? Why? Do you spend time around extended family out of choice or out of obligation, perhaps driven by cultural influences? Do you judge these people based on certain criteria and put your acquaintances in different circles of closeness around you? If so, what are those criteria that you judge? Do you uphold a different standard for your extended family members versus others?

2. How do you feel about people in the world, acquaintances, extended family, and friends?

Do you feel safe around them, or do you keep your antennae up at all times for signs of danger? Write both positive/pleasurable and negative/uncomfortable emotions. Notice your feelings about each of the groups. Do you feel you belong among them or not belong? Do you feel happy to imagine yourself among all these people, or do you feel angry or scared? Do you feel a connection with all your brothers and sisters out there on the planet, or do you feel very much alone? Do you feel relaxed or anxious? Do you have fun writing your Facebook postings, or do you fret over how you will come across and tailor your words to get the response you seek? Are your feelings different for each gender? If you have strong positive feelings about these friends, have you ever shared your feelings with them? If not, is this the time?

3. How do you behave toward people in the world, acquaintances, extended family, and friends?

As you capture your response to this question, you may find it interesting to check whether your behavior does or does not fit what you think and feel about those people all around you. Write both actions/behaviors that have created favorable results and ones that have created unfavorable results. If you responded earlier that you basically like people, do you now recognize that you speak freely to others and treat them with kindness and respect? If so, you have discovered a consistency between your thoughts/feelings and your behavior. However, if you said people are great, but now, upon reflection, you admit that you avoid eye contact with strangers, there's a conflict or disconnect there. That may be something you choose to reevaluate.

Of course, the inconsistency can run the other way. Let's say you acknowledged a belief that people are not to be trusted. Yet, as you think about your behavior toward people you don't know, you recognize that you feel safe around them. Perhaps you trust people more than you thought. This is useful information in gaining self-awareness, which is what this first area of life is all about. You are training yourself to become more self-aware.

When you attend a social gathering, do you always gravitate toward the "safe" friends or friendly faces, or do you allow yourself to approach new people? Does the company of others bring out the best in you, or do you feel on guard and conceal your true self?

This is where patterns may begin to emerge. Do you see equality in the friendships, or do you give more than you receive? Are you both there for each other? Do you both hold the friendship at the same level of importance? Observe the differences in your behavior with different groups of people you don't know, family, and friends, and notice the reason for these differences.

4. How does the way you think, feel, and behave toward people in the world, acquaintances, extended family, and friends impact your life and others' lives?

   Let's begin to make some connections. Write the positive and negative impacts. Perhaps you noted that you feel safe around people in the world. Now you consider how much you like to travel, and you can see how that attitude toward people helps open the door to enjoy new experiences. That's a nice confirmation that a particular attitude is serving you. On the flip side, you might now uncover an understanding of just how protective you are around people you don't know and that connects to your feeling that they can harm you. Maybe that protectiveness helped you avoid potential harm, but your constant need to protect yourself may be limiting your ability to get a better job or attract a mate.

   So, right from the start, you're beginning to see how you're responsible for how you think, feel, and behave with people. If you've been operating on automatic pilot, steered by outside influences, you can begin to adjust how you relate to the world. Maybe you notice how you judge people you don't know because of their culture or race or just because you see yourself as being in some "higher group." Now you can begin treating others as real people.

   Do you like the impact that your attitude creates on your life? Has it furthered your life? Has the impact held you back? Are you dissatisfied with the impact? How does your attitude impact their lives? Do you like the impact that you are having on people around you?

5. When people in the world, acquaintances, extended family, and friends are around you, what do you assume they think about you?

   Go ahead, write or speak your first thoughts, even if unflattering: "they think I'm ugly"; "they think I'm not very sophisticated"; or "they think I'm poor or lower than them." What you're capturing are mostly projections. After all, you don't know some of these people. And even if you do know them, they might have not said what they really think of you.

   Do you assume that they are judging you or that they accept/appreciate you? Do you assume they admire the way you live your life, or do they have judgments that they keep to themselves? To what extent do you care what these others around you really think about you?

   Many of our projections tend to be negative. That's perfectly natural. They are simply reflecting some way in which we may not accept ourselves. This piece of self-awareness may be something you can explore further as we go along. Of course, you may notice conversely that people seem to like you or think you're trustworthy. That response confirms something you may value about yourself. Either way, simply allow your answers to unfold.

6. When people in the world, acquaintances, extended family, and friends are around you, how do you assume they feel about you?

Do you assume they feel intimidated by you? Are they afraid of you? Or perhaps you imagine that people feel they can trust you. Consider that when you observe or project a particular feeling from people toward you, it affects your natural way of feeling toward them or your feeling toward yourself. For example, if you observe and assume that someone is afraid of you or is annoyed by you, what happens inside of you? What if you observed and assumed that they love you or care for you? How would that change your feelings about them or yourself?

Continue to respond openly and honestly. You don't need to make any conclusions, but if an "aha" is waiting to be grasped and put to good use, follow it. Sometimes their feelings may be very clear to you, but it's possible that your answers here may simply be projections. Even as projections, however, they offer clues as to how you see yourself. So welcome that form of awareness.

For some people, there is a gap between what they believe their friends feel about them and what they hope their friends feel about them. Pay attention to what is true for you.

7. When people in the world, acquaintances, extended family, and friends are around you, how do you experience their behavior toward you?

Do you notice that people come toward you, talk freely and openly, and tell their most intimate parts of their life? Or do they shy away and avoid looking at your eyes? Are they hostile toward you, or do they appear to be intruding in your space?

It's fine if your answer runs along the lines of "I don't even notice" or "they don't act any certain way toward me." There's no standard to meet in terms of how dramatic or revealing your responses should be. Many of us don't pay much attention to how strangers seem to perceive and act toward us, which may be a reflection of our confidence or self-esteem.

However, if you answer "I don't know," you can challenge yourself. Imagine that you're in your local Starbucks and you're looking at people's faces as they encounter you. Does the way they act appear to be consistent with what you suppose they're thinking about you? Again, your responses may simply be projections. It's eye opening to become aware of how our behavior toward other people is fueled by what we project as their attitude toward us. Sometimes we live in an imagined world and react to that world, which is really our own creation.

How your friends behave toward you is likely to be easier to track than pinning down their thoughts and feelings. You see their actions in the moment. So spend a little time sifting through the evidence. You may instantly zero in on the actions of one particular acquaintance or extended family member around you. Follow that trail, and then see what other relationships may be worth assessing here. Does their behavior represent what you had assumed they thought and felt about you? Is this similar to or different from how you behave toward them?

8. How has the way that you assume people in the world, acquaintances, extended family, and friends think, feel, and behave toward you impacted your life and others' lives?

Are you an attractive woman who recognizes how people pay more attention to you, or often approach you to speak? If so, do you relish that attention or simply accept it as part of human nature—especially male nature? Are you using this attention as a strategy to get ahead in life? Or does it leave you feeling bitter or cynical about being seen within a box, with others not paying attention to all those other parts of you? Have you lost opportunities in life due to these types of reactions? Or, if you believe people don't like you, has that prompted you to act in a shy manner around others? If so, how has that shyness held you back?

You may be surprised at how profound that impact may be here, well before we even reach your core relationships with your immediate family or your spouse. Perhaps you have identified a strength that has allowed you to attract friends who really do like you for who you are. So how can you tap that strength in other parts of your life? Or maybe you've seen that your circle of acquaintances could be wider if you can begin to let go of that fear of being judged. Being able to rely on close friendships often provides us a foundation for dealing with other more difficult or strained relationships. Is that part of your experience?

As you track your response, you may begin to see a firm statement about yourself constantly reemerging: "I don't belong" or "I'm less than those other people," for example. You may have fixated on this generalized belief and find that it extends to most areas of your life, forming the pillar of your identity. This is what we call a negative core belief.

Don't be alarmed if you see the makings of one or more negative core beliefs. You will soon learn how these beliefs usually emerge from a memory or experience when you were very young, and by exploring that triggering event you can release the emotions that cement the belief. Then you are free to counteract that belief. That's what we will be doing in a moment. But we've got some important questions to cover first.

9. When you are present with people in the world, acquaintances, extended family, and friends, what do you think about yourself?

   Maybe you'll respond with something such as, "I think the same way I usually do about myself: I'm basically a good person with strengths and weaknesses like everyone else." That's fine, and it may be all you want or need to say. But if you record an answer that sounds more like "I think I really am ugly," you have a choice. You can simply allow that answer to be, trusting that if it's a negative core belief driven by strong feelings it will come up to be examined soon enough. Or you can choose to challenge that thought by asking yourself, "Who told me that I'm ugly?" If you respond "no one, actually," you can explore where that belief came from and whether you already sense an opening to reframe it.

   Maybe being with these friends fills you with confidence, but perhaps you sometimes compare yourself to those friends. Is competition or jealousy a part of the picture here? Remember, this is where your core beliefs, either positive or negative, may begin to surface. Watch for phrases with a strong emotional tone: "I will never get anywhere" or "I think I'm a loser." That negative core belief is something you can explore when we get to the part about tracking and releasing emotions in this life area.

10. When you are present with people in the world, acquaintances, extended family, and friends, how do you feel about yourself?

    Perhaps you'll say, "I feel safe, secure, as if I belong; I feel I'm one with others in the world." Or maybe your response is, "I feel separate from others" or "I feel a sense of shame." Again, these are just your feelings about yourself, which you're simply gaining self-awareness about.

    Do you feel good about having a large number of friends and acquaintances to share time with, or do you feel a longing for a wider social circle to ward off a sense of alienation that sometimes comes upon you? Do you like your personality that emerges in social situations, or do you feel shame or embarrassment about it?

    For some people, being in the company of friends who care about them is reassuring or relaxing. For others, the accepting presence of a friend may open a door to deeper emotions that have been under the surface.

11. When you are present with people in the world, acquaintances, extended family, and friends, how do you behave toward yourself?

    Do you judge yourself? Do you punish yourself because you believe you don't measure up to the standards set by others? Or are you compassionate toward yourself, which leads you to be good at self-nurturing? Whatever it is that names how you behave toward yourself in this area, simply observe.

Perhaps your relationship with family members or friends will become more prominent here. Do you judge yourself for the way you behave toward certain members of your extended family or friends? Do you resent spending time with them, which you do out of a sense of duty? Or do you applaud yourself for maintaining ties where others you know have drifted apart from family and friends?

12. How does the way that you think, feel, and behave toward yourself when around people in the world, acquaintances, extended family, and friends impact your life and others' lives?

Perhaps you get depressed because you punish yourself. Or maybe the way you compare yourself negatively to others stops you from doing things you'd really like to do, such as launching a new career or sharing your passionate beliefs in a blog. Or maybe that core sense of connection you feel around other people is useful when you begin to feel a little down about something and you can just drive to a public park to gain comfort from being around humanity.

JENNIE'S STORY

Jennie, a twenty-five-year-old accountant, revealed a major problem with her social circle when she reached this area of the journey. It seemed that she recently had a falling out with a close friend and that friend started bad-mouthing her to other people in the same groups each belonged to. Jennie was so anxious about this blow to her reputation that she began having panic attacks. In our work, I helped her to identify the key phrase to track: This is unfair, and I am powerless to do anything about it. She discovered that her extreme fear stemmed from an experience in elementary school when girls would gossip about her and she wound up being scorned by others and ostracized from her most important groups. With this awareness, she followed the emotional-release process that you will be moving toward, and her fear cooled down. This emotional release opened the door for her to recognize that she did have control over her current situation. As one option, she knew that she could hire an attorney and explore a possible harassment suit against her former friend. She could also use this experience to evaluate how she chose her friends so that she would begin to make better decisions. Or she could simply adopt a stance toward such bad-mouthing that sounded something like this: It's just gossip. Who cares?

It can be helpful to look over your responses in this life area to pick out important points about the impact of your way of relating. If you find yourself mentioning more than once that "I'm not being myself around some of my friends and acquaintances," you may choose to ponder why that is true, what may be causing your inhibited behavior, and what changes you might like to make.

TRACKING AND RELEASING YOUR EMOTIONS

You now have a solid body of responses about your thoughts, feelings, and behavior related to people out there in the world that you know and don't know, friends, and extended family members. You have begun cultivating your self-awareness. The next step is to go back over your reflections and choose one of the more negative beliefs about yourself that you named. If you find more than one negative attitude, select the one phrase that most stands out because you feel a "charge" there or because you recognize it as part of a troublesome issue in your life. This will most likely represent your strongest negative core belief. Once you have chosen that phrase, "I am . . . ," write it down or speak it aloud again. You're going to do some further exploration.

Explore any emotion that may be operating with this negative core belief. Go back over your reflections, and state the negative belief that seems to have a particularly strong feeling behind it. Gently invite yourself to follow the emotion that arises from it as you state the negative belief.

So now, what voice do you hear reverberating from your responses that may in any way disturb or trouble you? Now is your chance to hear it more clearly and to see where it may lead you. Find that phrase or statement that had the biggest charge for you, the one that probably represents your negative core belief, and begin to track it now.

When you say "I am (fill in a negative belief about yourself from this section)," how does that make you feel? What is the emotion that arises when you say that belief to yourself?

If you chose "I don't belong" or "I'm no good," does that phrase bring up a feeling of sadness when you say it? Or is it anger? Something else? Take a moment to sift through what the emotion really is for you. Then simply note that feeling.

Where do you experience this feeling in your body? Is it in your head? Or is it in the muscles around your heart and chest area? Regardless of the area you sense this emotion, name it. Don't be concerned if you are having difficulty locating the emotion in your body. This is a skill you will be learning and practicing as we go along. To help with this first experience, ask yourself

REBECCA'S STORY

Rebecca was suffering anxiety and grief over the loss of her best friend. She and this other woman had been close for more than twenty years, going back to high school, and Rebecca was also close to her friend's mother. Recently this friend had pulled away, and Rebecca was frozen with the single question: Why? She certainly didn't believe she had done anything to deserve being dumped. Yes, she understood the concept of how people sometimes grow in different ways and friendships no longer fit, but emotionally she was hooked. Her negative core belief was, "I'm bad. This is all about me."

When Rebecca went into her feelings of sadness and shame, the memory that surfaced was a picture of how her mother had mistreated her. Because her mother did not mistreat her older sister in the same way, she internalized the belief that she was bad and that her mother's behavior was all about her as the daughter who didn't deserve love, rather than being an issue with her mother. She was able to gently release her feelings about this experience, recognizing that she really wasn't bad and undeserving of love. After we completed our work in this life area, she was not only able to look at the loss of this friendship in a new light (though it still hurt) but also able to recognize and validate the many other friendships she had maintained for twenty years or more. She took in all the love around her and embraced the truth that she deserved to have it.

whether you are feeling any general tension anywhere in your body. If so, work with that location. You can also simply repeat the phrase or sentence with the negative association again, and tell yourself to be fully present as you say it. Then scan your body from the top of your head all the way down to your toes, stopping to repeat the phrase again if needed. Most likely you will be able to identify a particular area of your body where that emotion resides. If not, just ride with the overall sensation of the feeling.

On a scale of zero to ten what is the intensity of that feeling?

If the intensity is very high and you assign it a ten, there's no need to be concerned. You will be having an experience with that feeling in a moment that should lead you to the origination of it or help you release it. And remember, emotions are just emotions. They often come and go like the rain. If you record your intensity as a one or two, perhaps you have a negative core belief that has no deep emotion behind it. It may not need releasing, only awareness. Whatever number fits your intensity of your feeling, record it at this time.

Close your eyes. Focus on the area of your body that you experience that feeling. Feel the emotion and allow it to take you with the muscles of your body to the first time you ever experienced this feeling and told yourself _____ (fill in the phrase with the negative belief about yourself).

It's okay if you're not sure if it was the first time you experienced that feeling and negative belief. Just trust that it's a memory that had an impact on formulating this belief.

Write down or speak out loud the first or earliest memory that appears.

Ask yourself the following: How old am I? Who is with me? What is happening? How do I react to it? The important part of the memory will likely be right there for you to look at.

As you see the younger you in the memory, how were you thinking about yourself at that time?

Notice if it was a new negative self-belief. How did the younger you feel about yourself? Where is this feeling in your body? What is the intensity from zero to ten?

Allow this feeling with the muscles of your body to take you to the first time you felt this kind of feeling and told yourself, "I am _____ (fill in the new negative self-belief)."

Open your eyes. Write down or speak this memory and what you found in visiting it. Write or speak your visual, auditory, and all-felt-sense memory.

Look over what you have uncovered about this memory again. As you focus on this memory, what do you think about the young you in the memory? How do you feel about the young you in the memory?

Perhaps in this memory you are imagining yourself as an eight-year-old girl. Your negative phrase was "I am no good," and the memory took you back to your mother shouting at you, or perhaps hitting you, for some simple misdeed. You can see that the little girl in the memory (you) feels sad or scared.

Ask the younger you in the memory what you need. Offer empathy and understanding related to that need. Validate that you as the child did not get what you needed at that time. Remind your child self that as a future version of that child you know you have survived the ordeal and are ready to take care of the child's emotional need, and that you are assessing as a grown-up how to fulfill what is needed now.

On a scale of zero to ten, what is the intensity of the felt feeling?

Now close your eyes and focus on the area of your body where you experience that feeling. Allow this experience in your body to take you again to the first time that you had a similar experience.

Write or speak the memory.

What is the intensity of the feeling from zero to ten now?

Breathe deeply. After a few moments, focus on that emotion and say to yourself, "release." Try to bring the intensity of the emotion as low as possible. Ask yourself, "As I look at myself with people in the world, what do I think and feel about myself?" Notice if a different negative core belief comes up. If yes, go through the process again. If neutral or positive beliefs surface, relax your breath and take a moment to simply rest. Then open your eyes.

Regardless of the number you name on the intensity scale, remember that those feelings and beliefs will likely show up again as you visit the next areas of life, so you can continue to work with them. Understand, however, that there is no need to set a goal to reduce your number to zero, one, or two. If you are responding to sadness from the death of your mother, for example, that feeling may never be fully released. A degree of sadness will likely always remain. What is important to recognize is that the past is the past. You can't change it. But you can change the meaning that you give to it and the impact of that meaning on your life.

The process of tracking emotions in this life area is one that you will follow when you work with negative core beliefs and charged feelings in each of the other life areas that you will be visiting on your Awareness Integration journey. You may not want or need to repeat each step, but you will always have this detailed map to refer to as a guide. The format of these questions also appears in appendix A for your easy reference.

Also, for each life area that you spend time tracking your emotions and negative core beliefs, keep in mind that you may need to consult a professional therapist whenever you access a strong emotion that you are not able to release or shake on your own. You may have come upon a trauma and may therefore need the attention and guidance of an expert to help you get through it. Do not hesitate to reach out for this kind of assistance at any time while you are following the Awareness Integration journey. Professional therapists are well equipped to help you follow your path of healing, growth, and change.

LAB WORK

Allow yourself to be present with the twelve questions of this area as you are living your daily life to gain more real-time awareness.

Hopefully you will find this homework easy and enjoyable. As you go into the world this week, spend some time observing what happens when you are around people that you do not know, acquaintances, friends, and family. What are you actually thinking and feeling? What do you suppose they are really thinking and feeling about you? What is your behavior toward these people? Is there a change that you would like to try in how you behave toward them?

After you've gathered your "data" from your lab work, be sure to bring it back to your Awareness Integration journal or recording. In doing so, you will be enhancing your growing ability to be truly self-aware.

Chapter Three

Career and Money

Most of us spend the majority of our waking hours working at our jobs or career. In many ways, our work or career may define who we are and how we live. Our attitude toward our work life and the energy we invest in it often has a carry-over effect on other parts of our life, including our closest relationships.

In this area, I invite you to focus on two primary goals: (1) gain awareness of who you are in your job or career and with money; and (2) gain awareness of your feelings linked to that identity and its impact on you. Before you begin to respond to the core questions, it may help to ask yourself some initial questions to prime your awareness pump.

Are you what you do? What does the term "career" mean to you? Is your idea of career and a job aligned with a commitment to create the life you really want to live, or does it reflect an attitude that work is just something you have to do to get by? Are you currently engaged in a "job" or a calling? Is there or has there been some other career that you wanted to follow but were unable to bring to fruition?

Are you passionate about your work, often going beyond what is expected? Or do you just put in your eight hours and try to look busy, approaching your job as a means to survive, much like an animal has to produce to eat? If you do hold a job just for survival, you may have a passion about a career that has not been unleashed. When you don't feel passion, it can lead to acting impulsively with negative results that can trickle down to other parts of your life. For example, if you routinely lie about your activities at your job, you may bring that into a pattern of lying at home.

When I work with clients on this area of the Awareness Integration journey, I often ask them, Do you experience yourself as an employee, a manager, or an owner? Some of that identification comes from an external role or definition, but that doesn't tell the whole story of how engaged we are in our work. Much of that definition is internal. Someone who sweeps the floors of a large store might carry such a positive attitude that, with every sweep, he is making the statement, "I own this damn place!"

If you don't currently have a career or a significant job, the same kinds of questions can be relevant if you are pursuing an education. Are you just in school because you have to earn some degree or certification in order to achieve your career goals, or are you fully invested in the process of learning? If you're attending college and you're not sure what career track to pursue, do you evaluate your options from the perspective of what will pay the bills or from reflecting on what is in you that is really a gift to put into motion to serve others and the larger world?

So your "job" in this life area is to explore your attitudes related to these kinds of issues. And as with all the other areas, you are also on the lookout for strong feelings that may be tracked and released, to gain more freedom over how you approach your work . . . and your life.

Your job or career lives within a community of coworkers, colleagues, managers, bosses, employers, employees, and customers. As you consider your identity in this arena, and go on to name your thoughts, feelings, and behavior, many possible issues may emerge.

For example, do you find yourself consistently trying to compete against your coworkers, or are you more of a team player? If you are competitive, what is your style? Are you constantly strategizing or concocting new schemes to get ahead, carrying an attitude similar to an animal on the hunt where you're just waiting to put your foot down on your victim, raise your fist, and shout "Yeah!" Or do you adopt a more passive-aggressive style, working behind the scenes with a smirk that says, "Ha, ha, no one knows what I'm up to!"

I often find with my clients that their need to compete and the manner in which they do it can be traced back to sibling rivalries. If you felt you needed to compete for love and attention at home, maybe you have brought that attitude into your workplace persona. On the other hand, if you were a people pleaser at home, you may feel threatened by others who relentlessly compete at work. If so, how do you respond to what you see? Do you complain to your boss about the coworker who comes in late and makes private phone calls on work time?

If you're a team player, do you tend to be a leader or a follower? Do you need to show that you are the best at any task or assignment, sometimes doing whatever you think you need to do even though it means pushing others aside? Or do you blend your talents to make the team stronger? If you assume the identity of a team leader, does the evidence from those around you support your belief? Or does it indicate instead that you are just pretending to be a leader, with no real followers?

In regard to relationships at work, how do you handle gossip about your bosses or coworkers? Do you sometimes initiate it or spread it when it starts, or do you condemn it and refuse to participate? How do you respond when the gossip is about you?

How do you make friends among your pool of colleagues and coworkers? Do you connect with people out of some shared interest in life, or do you just get together to whine and complain about work? Do you support your friends in their career, or do you use these connections to advance your own cause?

If you work from home, how do you discipline and structure yourself? How do you communicate and connect with your coworkers? Do you feel free by doing work at home? Do you feel more stressed by getting interrupted by matters that happen at home?

If your career is a homemaker, how do you define your career from your behavior as a family member? What constitutes work and what constitutes your home task? What job description, duties, and responsibilities do you assign to your career, and which do you expect your mate to equally contribute to? Who would you consider your coworkers or colleagues? Other homemakers?

What about flirting at work? Do you initiate it or at least respond to it, or do you distance yourself from that kind of activity? As we all know, many romantic relationships are formed among coworkers and colleagues, and sometimes one or both partners are already married. I had a female client who engaged in mutual flirting with a man she saw regularly at work. They complained about each other's spouses and otherwise explored common ground. She loved the connection, but for years she held back on further romantic involvement—until both divorced their spouses. So of course she rushed right into a "real" relationship with this guy, and surprise, their relationship instantly began to look and feel very different. Instead of complaining about their spouses, they were soon complaining about each other! They had fantasized about each other as partners, but the fantasy wasn't real.

Of course, you may be married to the person you work with, perhaps running a business together. If so, you can spend additional time looking at that relationship through the lens of being coworkers. Do you bring your work home and approach your home life as if you're still in a business meeting? Or are you able to carve out time and space just for each other as life partners? In assisting couples who operate a business together, one of my first suggestions is to take the time to create specific job descriptions for each partner in order to head off unnecessary power struggles on the job. They may have enough of that at home already!

By the way, if you are your own boss in the work that you do, you will probably need to shift some of the terms we are using here. Consider the full spectrum of relationships that you may have with managers, employees, colleagues, and clients. Even if you work alone, somehow or other you spend time relating to other people in the work that you do. This is your opportunity to explore those relationships and see what you can learn from them.

Many of us have found ourselves caught in a moment of recognition when we are looking at our boss or authority figure as the "Good Daddy" or the "Good Mommy," or the "Bad Daddy" or the "Bad Mommy." It is almost inevitable that at some time or another we make an association with the person in charge at our workplace with those who were in charge of us growing up. Gaining awareness of this dynamic, if applicable, stands as one of many important possibilities for growth as you visit this area of life.

The similarities between bosses and parents are obvious. Either party can hold us or scold us, though the "holding" at work is usually more metaphoric than literal. They can say "good job" or tell us when we have messed up and what we need to do about it. A boss can take away the source of your finances, just as your mother can take away the source of your milk. It's a powerful position to be in, and with either party we may resent this power. We may see our boss as having more power, in fact, because while our parents could punish us, they couldn't fire us. We may act fearful of our boss wielding the ax, and then flip to anger that this person should have so much control over our fate.

While responding to the questions in this life area, it may be helpful to look for projections. Have you labeled your boss as that "Good Mommy" and begun to share your personal problems with her? When she sets a boundary appropriate to her role, you may find yourself thinking, "You can't do that! You're my good mommy!" Conversely, if your boss has become the "Bad Daddy" to you, similar to your father with whom you were in conflict, you may purposely look for and overreact to any shred of evidence that confirms this "daddy" boss is mean and unfair.

Your issues with your boss may not directly connect to your parents, but consider whether you responded to any or most authority figures with a rebel stance. You may recognize here that when it comes to perceiving and relating to bosses, you have followed the unspoken words, "This is an authority figure, so I must rebel against him (or her)." If so, ask yourself how well this posture is working for you.

Maybe you're not the rebel but rather the "good child" who follows all the rules from above and never questions authority, no matter what that person in the role of authority may do. Once you gain awareness of playing this role, you may discover that you have more freedom to act in a more balanced and authentic way around your bosses.

Notice also whether you have any tendency to blame your boss for your own failures or shortcomings. Is there a way to begin taking more responsibility for what you do and where you are going in your career?

If you are your own boss, feel free again to shift the wording around to make this life area relevant to your situation. Most of us have some kind of "boss" or authority figure to report to. You can focus on that person or group of individuals. Or you can address the questions toward that part of you that happens to be a boss.

1. What do you think of your career, job, or education? Coworkers, colleagues, boss, authorities in general, and employees?

   Write both positive and negative thoughts. "I think my career perfectly fits who I am," or "I think my job is hell." Note your strongest beliefs, whatever they happen to be.

   Right from the outset here, you may find yourself making observations about your attitude toward your fellow workers in general, but then zero in on one or two challenging or impactful relationships. Feel free to go in that direction if that's what is calling for your attention.

   A word of caution: If you are following the Awareness Integration journey on your laptop, make sure you are using a program that ensures this information will remain safely out of the hands of anyone at work! Once you feel confident that you are protected, tell the truth of what you think and why. Rather than get too caught up with assessing your boss's performance, you may want to tighten your inquiry to focus primarily on how your boss relates to you.

2. How do you feel about your career, job, or education? Coworkers, colleagues, boss, authorities, and employees?

   Do you love it or merely tolerate it? Do you feel sad or angry about putting aside your true goals, or do you feel gratitude for having your dream job? Notice how your feelings may be emerging right away when you say or write things such as, "I feel hopeless about my situation, and I know it will never change." You will have the opportunity to just feel that emotion and invite a release of it in a few moments.

3. How do you behave toward your career, job, or education? Coworkers, colleagues, boss, authorities, and employees?

   Do you approach it with full gusto or something much less? Are you fully yourself or some kind of actor? Do you seek your boss's attention or try to avoid it?

4. How does the way you think, feel, and behave toward your career, job, education, coworkers, colleagues, boss, authorities, or employees impact your life and others' lives?

Consider each question carefully, and then respond as honestly as you can. Again, there is no "correct" way to look at the work you do, only what is right for you within the life you choose to live.

If you routinely bring home your attitudes and feelings about your boss, your spouse could no doubt help you answer this question! Be on the lookout also for positive ways that your boss and the way you deal with that person are influencing your life.

Maybe you have learned how to become more accountable in everything you do. You can also assess how your way of being affects your boss.

5. What do you assume people who are related to your work think about you?

How do you assume your coworkers think about you? Your boss? I bet some of your family or friends have strong opinions about your approach to your career, even telling you what you should be doing. Give voice to those thoughts and opinions here. Their attitudes may or may not be accurate, at least in your eyes, but they most likely influence you in some way. Seek to go beyond the tangible evidence of job evaluations, promotions, bonuses, or raises. What do you imagine they think about you as a person?

6. What do you assume people who are related to your work feel about you?

Perhaps they admire you, or you assume that they fear you. Don't forget to include your own reaction to whatever your coworkers and colleagues feel about you. Be honest.

If your boss tells you she likes you, do you believe her or do you doubt her? What part of your answer has to do with that person, and what part has to do with you?

Do they feel angry that you're not making needed changes? Do they envy you, or do they feel sorry for you? Remember, when you do your lab work for this area of life you can ask them!

7. How do people who are related to your work behave toward you?

Do they give you concrete advice? Do they avoid talking about your work at all, and if so, what do you imagine that means? Do you listen to it or reject it? Regardless of the behavior, do you take it personally? If so, might there be a different perspective waiting for you to tap into?

8. How has the way that you assume people who are related to your work think, feel, and behave toward you in relation to your job or career impacted your life and others' lives?

Maybe you realize that you only chose your career because it was what your parents wanted you to do. Or perhaps you became determined to do the opposite. Then again, perhaps you have always been able to tune out the input from other people and have stuck to doing the work that you believe is right for you. Regardless of your experience, write it down here.

Perhaps any negative judgments you receive at work have no effect on you because you have a sturdy self-identity or because others who love you validate your true nature. Good for you! But if you know that those people at work do influence you, take an honest look at how that is true.

9. In the area of work and career, what do you think about yourself?

This is where your responses may begin to shift from just capturing attitudes about your work to identifying attitudes about yourself. Watch for those emotionally charged phrases: "My work enables me to make a contribution to the world" or "I'm a sellout!" Those are the kinds of phrases that may signal a major negative core belief.

They may sound something like "I am competent," "I am better than them," "I am smart," or "I am less than/not good enough/not liked." Perhaps you think you've got the best workplace environment in town. If so, explain why. Or if being at your workplace leaves you constantly thinking how you need to get out of there in order to maintain your sanity, give voice to that attitude. Do you think you're foolish for worrying how they perceive you? Do you ever secretly believe you are superior to them? Again, watch for negative core beliefs: "I think I'm inept," "I'm in a hole I will never climb out of," "I need a new career," and so forth.

10. In the area of work and career, how do you feel about yourself?

Do you feel great satisfaction or deep frustration? Do your feelings change from day to day? If so, what circumstances trigger the shift? Do you feel you're a fool to be doing work that's beneath you, or do you salute yourself for remaining dedicated to your long-term career goals? Make note of your discoveries without making yourself wrong for what you feel. If you feel inferior, you may be shielding that insecurity from your coworkers. But you can't hide it from yourself.

The voices may reflect thoughts of "I'm not enough" or "This isn't fair!" Listen to those voices, and write down their messages. Does this make you feel angry, shameful, empty, or sad?

11. In the area of work and career, how do you behave toward yourself?

Write your positive and negative behavior. Would you say that you act authentically while at your job, or do you try to look good? Your coworkers and colleagues may not see you retreating from a strained work encounter, talking to yourself about how to hatch your next plot to look good. But if it is happening, give yourself permission to acknowledge that here. This is all about gaining awareness of your life.

Do you push yourself in a harsh manner because you've got to keep up, or do you nurture yourself properly? Do you judge yourself or get angry at yourself and your coworkers? Do you scold yourself with every mistake that you make? Do you praise and reward yourself? Do you chastise yourself for doing a lousy job? Do you comfort yourself with a vision of life with the next boss?

12. How does the way that you think, feel, and behave toward your self in the area of work and career impact your life and others' lives?

Write the positive and negative impact.

Again, our working life in many ways defines us. It's natural that the way we are at work extends into the way we are in our lives to some degree. Take inventory of how and where that may be true for you and what the impact looks like. More importantly, consider whether that impact is something you approve of or something you would like to change. If you are telling yourself, "Be careful, walk on tiptoes," around your boss, do you follow that same guiding voice around your mate, your children, or the customer service representative giving you the runaround? Look for any carry-over behavior that you might like to let go of.

Another question that I ask my clients is, "If you didn't have to worry about feeding your family or other financial responsibilities, if you didn't have to worry about upsetting others, what would you do just because you were natural at it and felt excited about doing it?" One of my male clients had an instant response.

"Oh, I would just play golf all the time," he said.

"That's awesome," I replied. "Why not try to find a way to do it?"

That's when the emotion behind his statement surfaced. He felt shame because all his siblings were attorneys or other professionals. Because he had not risen to that level, he carried the negative core belief "I'll never be good enough." I assisted him in exploring that feeling, which he traced to childhood. After releasing that feeling, he was able to let go of that limiting, negative core belief. That's when he began to allow his gift to come out. Before long, he became manager of a golf course. "I feel like I'm in heaven!" he said. Of course, he also had to develop some new practical skills to get moving in this new direction.

Many times our struggles and frustration in any life area stem from a lack of the skills that we need to handle something in a different way or take a step in an exciting new direction. As you will discover on the second phase of your journey, Awareness Integration will provide you with an opportunity to identify new goals in many realms of your life and cultivate the concrete skills needed to bring those goals to fruition.

If you're carrying a negative belief about yourself in the area of work or career, a statement that most stirs your feelings, now is your chance to see what's behind it.

One client focusing on this area of the model revealed that she spent 80 percent of her time and energy at work studying other people's reactions to her. Any time she saw them laughing or talking together, she always said, "It must be about me!" This attitude impacted how she performed her job. Her company had a rule that when a call from a customer came in, you had to answer by the second ring.

Failure to do so could mean losing your job. With the first ring my client would look around and notice others not responding. Feeling anxious, she would pick up on the second ring but resented doing it. At first she insisted to me that this happened all the time, but later she admitted that it was only about one-third of the time.

It was clear that negative core beliefs, driven by strong emotions, were at play. She found herself proclaiming, "I'm not good enough. People don't accept me. They talk behind my back all the time." Feelings of shame came to the surface. Under that she found sadness as well as anger. We traced these feelings to a childhood dynamic in which three of her cousins, all sisters, would routinely put her down or leave her out. Revisiting that memory helped her to release the sadness and anger and come away with a new meaning. Before long, she was able to say, "I am good enough" and stopped projecting the reactions of her coworkers. She even went back for further job training and qualified for much better jobs in much healthier work environments.

So is there a negative statement or belief that cropped up while you were responding to the questions of this area? Do you seem to have an intense feeling associated with that belief? If so, follow the steps that will help escort you through the terrain of seeing an associated feeling, releasing the emotion, and opening the door to potential changes.

So as you look for your more "charged" findings in your responses here, you may similarly discover that awareness is enough to ignite a positive change. Or you may indeed be sitting on an emotional hot spot that you sense was triggered by your relationship with a parent or some experience in your past. So this is your opportunity to track that experience, because it may enable you to tap into a negative core belief. Go to appendix A for the complete exercise.

MONEY

The product of your career or job is money and wealth. However, the identity that you hold with your careers might be different than the one you hold with money and wealth.

"Money is the root of all evil." "Money is all there is." "Money is just a tool for living a good life." "All wealthy people are greedy." "With wealth there is an open ceiling as to how much you can obtain." "The idea of ever getting rich today is just a fantasy because the system is stacked against us."

Do any of those beliefs or messages resonate with you? Do you carry a different attitude about money and its role in your life? Let's uncover and examine your own concepts and beliefs about one subject that everyone seems to deal with every day. Our thoughts, feelings, and behavior toward money and wealth are in the air almost constantly, so by taking the time to grasp those influences you will be pulling in more and more clues about what drives your life and how and where you may want to shift gears.

Take a few moments to consider some of the dominant messages about money you have heard and followed. Then ask the important follow-up question: "Where did I get those messages?" Did your parents instill in you a belief that you had to obtain wealth to reach or maintain a certain status? Did you plug into a cultural message about money being a means to happiness? Think about not only those messages you have embraced but also those you have rebelled against. Perhaps you rejected the notion that money is meant to be hoarded so you've dedicated much of your life to sharing what you have with others.

What is your style with money and wealth? Are you planning for the future, or do you live for today? Are you constantly worrying about having enough, or do you trust that somehow it will all be all right? Do you yearn to follow the model of those wealthier than you, or do you rage against them and what they did to get there? Do you blame the government or the economy for staying stuck in the middle of the money spectrum?

When I guide clients in this life area, passionate beliefs and strong emotions often surge forward quickly. A male client admitted to a belief that he didn't deserve to have much money and felt hopeless about that. A woman touched upon her sadness over not having as much money as she wanted and then shifted to feeling angry about that. In both situations, simply bringing attention to the feelings that got stirred allowed them to dissipate as they continued along on their journey.

With another woman working the model, a sense of anxiety about tumbling into poverty surfaced. This was a professional woman, making good money, but she had never bought her own home and refused to spend anything on herself. When we tracked her belief that drove the anxiety, she discovered that she had taken on her father's fear of losing his money. That belief she held to so tightly wasn't hers at all. Just making this discovery cleared the space for her to proclaim, "I deserve to spend money!" She soon began enjoying doing things just for herself.

This kind of experience may happen often for you while following the Awareness Integration trail: You tap into a negative core belief, you track its influence, and you learn that you've been carrying someone else's attitude along with you like dead weight. The awareness of this reality itself can set you free.

You may find that your beliefs and attitudes about money have changed and evolved over the years. I had the humbling experience of only waking up to the importance of saving for the future when I was closing in on my fiftieth birthday. Before then, my mantra was "make money, spend money." So you might take stock of what you believed about money when you were younger and what you believe today.

Are you ready to roll the dice on your thoughts, feelings, beliefs, and behavior related to money and wealth?

1. What do you think about money and wealth?

    Do you have a cap for the wealth that you believe you deserve? Do you have a positive attitude toward one group who has wealth versus the ones that don't? What is the figure and lifestyle that you call wealth? Do you have a wealthy attitude while the earning is not high or have a scarcity and poverty attitude although the earning power and lifestyle is higher than the average? Explore both the negative and positive thoughts you are experiencing.

2. How do you feel about money and wealth?

    Do you feel proud, competent, and happy when you have money? Or feel embarrassed, guilty, and ashamed? Do you feel fear, anxiety, and anger when you are short of money? Do you feel angry or envious of other's wealth? What feelings, both negative and positive, surface when you think about money and the effect it has on your life and views of yourself?

3. How do you behave toward money and wealth?

    A quick peek at your checking account balance or credit card statement might offer some clues about your management of money. Do you borrow money, or is it against your values? Do you lend money to others? Do you contribute to a church or a nonprofit organization? Do you lecture about money to others? Do you need to be in control of money, or would you prefer others to control and manage the money for you? Do you purchase name-brand objects to show that you are affluent? Or do you purposely dress down so that people don't know about your wealth?

CASSANDRA'S JOURNEY

Cassandra, a woman whom I assisted, admitted that she only valued and wanted to be around rich people. And yet this brought out a conflict for her because deep inside she believed she was not good enough to fit in with people who had lots of money and followed a certain lifestyle. Her negative core belief was, "I'm not good enough!" When we traced her feelings back to childhood, Cassandra remembered how her mother had wanted her to marry a rich husband and so had sent her to expensive private schools and social gatherings of the wealthy. It turns out that her mother had risen up from poverty and so naturally wanted her daughter to follow the same path, and the only way she believed that could happen was by being Cinderella waiting for the prince to show up.

But Cassandra didn't really want to play Cinderella at all. She actually believed in the idea that a modern marriage should be between two equals. She had simply taken on her mother's shame and strife. After spending time simply being present with her feelings about this conflict, she was more than ready to let go of her mother's influence. She soon found herself saying things like, "I'll create my own wealth my own way, and I won't force myself where I don't belong." And she believed it!

4. How does the way you think, feel, and behave toward your money and wealth impact your life and others' lives?

    Keep in mind that this question is not simply asking about how your personal financial status impacts your life. It invites a full inquiry as to how you think, feel, and act toward that status. How do you control other people's money? How does your earning capacity or how you manage money impact other people's life?

5. What do you assume people think about you in the area of creating and managing money?

    In the area of earning and managing money, do others see you as greedy? Or do they think you're the most generous person they know? Do they think you pay too much attention to money or not enough? Do they think you control them with money or control their management of money?

6. What do you assume people feel about you in the area of creating and managing money?

    Do you sense that they are proud of you? Envy you? Are angry with you? Are jealous of you? Feel pity for you? Feel compassionate toward you?

7. How do you assume people behave toward you in the area of creating and managing money?

   Do they ask to borrow money? Do they get your advice about money and wealth? Do they refrain from talking about money to you?

8. How does the way you assume people think, feel, and behave toward you in the area of money and wealth impact your life and others'?

   If you assume others think of you as a wealthy person, does that force you or inspire you to keep the success going? Do you have to keep a facade to prove something to others about your money or wealth?

9. In relation to money and wealth, what do you think about yourself?

   Do you think to yourself, "I am competent," "I am clueless," "I am responsible and accountable," or "I am not enough"? Write both positive and negative beliefs about yourself.

10. In relation to money and wealth, how do you feel about yourself?

    Would you say, "I feel proud," "I feel shame," "I feel grateful and blessed," or "I feel miserable and angry at myself for being lazy"?

11. In relation to money and wealth, how do you behave toward yourself?

    Do you spend money on yourself freely and feel good about it? Do you scold yourself for spending? Do you manipulate yourself to buy something that you can't afford? When you see your Visa balance, do you rush for the ice cream or potato chips to avoid thinking about or dealing with it? Do you chastise yourself for frivolous spending, or give yourself credit for showing your restraint? Maybe the act of looking at your current financial status just makes you feel stuck.

12. In relation to money and wealth, how does the way you think, feel, and behave toward yourself affect your and other people's lives?

    Does it move you forward in your life, or has your attitude toward yourself made you stuck in a rut? If you have a generally positive relationship with money and wealth, does that extend into the rest of your life? If so, great! You're probably ready to move on to the next area of life. However, if you have uncovered important issues and charged feelings, spending time looking at them here could potentially open the door to significant change.

Let's explore where your strongest feelings and negative core beliefs will lead you in this arena. If you say, "I am poor and will never get out of this mess," you may ignite feelings of sadness, resentment, and shame. Go to appendix A for the complete exercise.

Chapter Four

Just a Bit Closer

In this chapter you'll explore three different groups of people: your siblings, a significant person who has powerfully impacted your life, and your in-laws. Though they may not seem to have much in common at first glance, each group has a significant impact in your life. Even if you don't have any in-laws.

YOUR SIBLINGS

Your Awareness Integration journey is about to take a turn into your more formative relationships, those with your siblings and your parents. Most likely, you've got a wide spectrum of attitudes and experiences to draw from in these life areas. So buckle up for the ride!

Before we begin, you may want to take a moment to simply appreciate and reflect on the depth of awareness that you have already gained while exploring other relationships that are not necessarily rooted in childhood. That's the beauty of working with the Awareness Integration Model: You have opportunities to expand your awareness, release stored emotions that have blocked your path, and make positive changes in your life before you even focus on what you may consider your "core" relationships. You have been making that happen by your willingness to dive into each new area that we have been visiting.

So apply that same willingness and commitment now as you sink into your thoughts, feelings, and behavior toward your siblings. Consider first some of the basics: How many siblings do you have, and where are you in birth order in your family? Do you also have stepbrothers and stepsisters, or children you lived with when your parents divorced and created a merged family with a

43

new spouse? Which siblings did you align with or get along best with? Which sibling relationships created conflict? Did you feel more comfortable with siblings closest to you in age, or to a brother or sister much older or much younger? Have your relationships with your siblings changed and evolved over the years, and if so, how were you able to steer those changes? If you have remained stuck in the same old struggles, why have you not been able to break up old patterns, and what has been the cost?

As you consider how well you have gotten along with your siblings, pay attention to the influence of your parents on these relationships. Were you the favored child, or was it a sibling? Did you get all the love and attention as the oldest but then lose that status when a younger sibling came along? How did these dynamics stay with you? Maybe you were the second child and believed that your older sibling was more powerful in the family system, prompting you to adopt a belief that "I'm nothing" or "I'm invisible," which has carried over into your adult life. Or maybe you got more attention than one or all of your siblings but feel guilty about that. If so, did you become hypervigilant about shying away from the spotlight during childhood and still do that today?

Our responses to what was present in our lives related to our siblings often show up as automatic thoughts, feelings, and behavior with friends, coworkers, or other important people in our adult life. All that sibling "stuff" gets replayed, and it may have been flying under the radar of your awareness for many years. Even if we have been in therapy, sometimes we get so narrowly focused on tracing our relationships with our parents and the impact that had on us that we forget to consider the effects that our connections with our siblings have had. Now is the time to shine the spotlight in that direction.

As you approach the questions related to this life area, it may be especially helpful to consider each sibling individually. In other words, you can choose to answer all the questions for one sibling before going through the questions again for your next sibling. Of course, if you came from a large family, it could take you a long time to move through the list! It's fine to select a smaller number of siblings to zero in on, starting with those with whom you have had the more involved relationships. Then you can go through the list responding to the questions as they relate to your siblings taken as a group.

Remember that the issues you bring forward in this exploration may well have been set in motion by trauma. You were young and vulnerable when these sibling bonds were being forged, and your parents were likely involved. There may be abuse in your picture, deep feelings of betrayal, or other impactful emotions. Whether the trauma that you uncover is known or new, it will be beneficial to make time and space for feeling those emotions and tracking them.

1. What do you think of your siblings?

   Again, you may want to begin by naming just one sibling and working through the questions with that person in mind. Then come back to this starting point for the next sibling. Maybe you think that one of your siblings has it easy in life and another sibling has it hard. Perhaps you think a sibling is stuck and will never change what needs attention in his or her life.

   You may have had a different thought process or relation with each one of your siblings when you were a child versus how is it today now that you are all adults. Try to express both time periods so that you get more information and can identify any process of change.

2. How do you feel about your siblings?

   Write both positive/pleasurable and negative/uncomfortable emotions. If you have at least two siblings, it's quite likely that you feel differently toward each one. Sort out those feelings as you work with these questions. It's also useful to distinguish whether these feelings were present with you when you were a child and remain with you today, or whether you feel differently after the years have gone by.

3. How do you behave toward your siblings?

   Write both actions/behaviors that have created favorable results and ones that have created unfavorable results. Do you play a very specific role with that sibling, such as the protective older brother or the deferring younger sister? How well does that role work or not work for you?

4. How does the way you think, feel, and behave toward your siblings impact your life and others' lives?

   You may be tempted to declare, "I don't see my siblings nearly as often now as I did when I was young, so it really doesn't matter." But even if you have less contact with your siblings, you still may be carrying the effects of what has transpired between you. Look closely.

5. When your siblings are around you, what do you assume they think about you?

   With most sibling relationships, we know what our brothers and sisters think of us because they tell us. But maybe you still find yourself guessing and wondering. Explore this and allow those thoughts to surface.

6. When your siblings are around you, how do you assume they feel about you?

   Write your positive and negative assumptions. Do they still feel jealous about something from long ago? Are they less tolerant of the differences between you now that you have grown in different directions? Or has a channel of love remained open?

7. When your siblings are around you, how do you experience their behavior toward you?

    Sometimes their behavior most shows itself in how interested they are to have contact with you. You may also be reacting to things such as whether or not you receive birthday calls or cards from them, or whether they seem to care about your children as much as you would want.

8. How has the way that you assume your siblings think, feel, and behave toward you impacted your life and others' lives?

    Maybe you have had a major breakup with a sibling because the negative impact was more than you wanted to bear. How has that split influenced you?

9. When you are present with your siblings, what do you think about yourself?

    Does being around them change the way you view yourself? "I am better and more competent than," "I am less than," or "I will never be loved by them."

10. When you are present with your siblings, how do you feel about yourself?

    Don't be surprised if many feelings rise to the surface, especially as you go through the relationship with each sibling individually. Do your best to follow along with all the emotional responses.

11. When you are present with your siblings, how do you behave toward yourself?

    Some people say they just "disappear" when they find themselves in a family gathering with their siblings. The pain from the past is something they'd rather not face. Does that ever happen to you? Or do you have the different experience of truly acting yourself around one particular brother or sister because that person knows you so well? Do you fall back into traditional roles? Do you judge yourself for how you treat them?

12. How does the way that you think, feel, and behave toward your siblings impact your life and others' lives?

    Write the positive and negative impact. As we discussed, you may want to consider whether sibling issues have become entangled with your relationships with other people. If they have, what might you do to lessen that influence?

As you see a negative core belief with a "charge," go to appendix A for the complete exercise.

FARA'S STORY (PART 1)

When my client Fara was taking the Awareness Integration journey, many strong feelings emerged when she was reflecting on her relationship with her younger twin sisters. One of those sisters really pushed her buttons!

She would often get angry in dealing with her, and under the anger she would access guilt. After all, from a very young age she had been assigned the role of taking care of those younger sisters, which meant submerging her own needs and feelings in order to fulfill her mission. Not surprisingly, this was a role that caused her great conflict and turmoil.

"I needed somebody to take care of me!" she shouted. "I felt so lonely." Her sadness bubbled over, and she pinpointed it as being centered in her throat. I invited her to gently be present with that sadness as she surveyed her childhood landscape for memories triggering this response. Many memories rushed to the forefront, most related to her father who struggled with depression and would swear that he just wanted to die. The crisis in her family and the burdens she was made to carry had taken its toll.

This was not news to Fara, but in working with Awareness Integration in this life area she was at least able to release some of the "juice" from those painful feelings. She experienced her sadness easing somewhat, and the guilt as well, so she could be more present in her adult relationships.

A MOST SIGNIFICANT PERSON IN YOUR LIFE

Most of us have benefited from the contributions of a significant person who was pivotal in our life as more of a motivational or inspirational figure. This is your time to bring him or her into the field of your awareness.

Often this significant person arrives in our life when we're beyond early childhood, perhaps during our teen or young adult years. Often the other person is a teacher or mentor. Sometimes it may be a parent of one of our friends, someone who appears more capable of role-modeling how to be an adult and how to guide a family than our own parents. Somehow or other, this person just seemed to carry some body of knowledge about a particular realm of life, or maybe all of life, that pulled us in. More important, that person seemed genuinely interested in us and was willing to go the extra mile in teaching or guiding us.

Who was it that stepped in to guide or inspire you? Was it an adult who seemed to have all the answers? Did you look at this person's life and say, "I want to be just like that?" Or was it more of a big brother or big sister type, someone only a little older than you but with greater maturity and a keen sense for who you were and what you needed?

What was it specifically that this person believed, did, or said that gave you a new perspective? What were the skills that you learned from the relationship? I had a friend who was raised by parents with little formal education. He was a shy boy who didn't really believe in himself. During high school, his physics teacher stirred his intellectual curiosity and an excitement for physics, while also providing true love and caring. As a result of this relationship, his confidence soared, and he went on to become an award-winning physicist.

One consideration to explore is whether your significant person filled a void, as it did for my friend, or whether that person simply helped steer you toward the next level of your growth. You also may want to reflect on how long the relationship lasted. Our significant person's active presence in our life may be quite brief, even a matter of months or a year or two. Still, when this kind of relationship ends, we may grieve it as deeply as losing a family member.

This relationship with a significant person is usually built with few expectations, unlike our bond with our parents. From our parents, we expect ongoing love, care, support, nurturance, and a constant presence. This connection with a significant person is the kind of relationship that usually just happens in its own beauty. It wasn't planned or scripted. It probably was not expected, and we didn't know what we would gain from it at first. Then—whatever this person gave us—we received it as a gift, with gratitude. Maybe that gift has come back to you later in life when you least expected it. See what your exploration into this relationship may reveal for you now.

1. What do you think of this significant person in your life?

    If you respond, "He was great," make sure to explain why. The more you bring out, the greater your awareness will be of the true impact of this relationship on your life.

2. How do you feel about this significant person in your life?

    Write both positive/pleasurable and negative/uncomfortable emotions. If you felt joy and appreciation, did you get an opportunity to express those feelings to this person?

3. How do you behave toward this significant person in your life?

   Write both actions/behaviors that have created favorable results and ones that have created unfavorable results. Did you sometimes act spellbound by what this person knew or how they approached life? Did you listen and pay attention as you never had with anyone else before?

4. How does the way you think, feel, and behave toward this significant person in your life impact your life and others' lives?

   While these relationships are often short term, their impact may extend for many years. See how you can track that influence in your situation. And if this significant person is still present in your life, how has that impact evolved?

5. When this significant person in your life is around you, what do you assume he or she thinks about you?

   Even if this person is deceased or far away, how do you think he or she would react to seeing how far you've come in your life?

6. When this significant person in your life is around you, what do you assume he or she feels about you?

   Is this person proud or pleased? Did your significant person get a chance to express those feelings to you?

7. When this significant person was/is around you, how do you experience his or her behavior toward you?

   Did this person approach you with a certain kind of knowing of who you really are? Did this person seem to regard you as the most important person in the world?

8. How has the way that you assume this significant person in your life thinks, feels, and behaves toward you impacted your life and others' lives?

   Often our achievements are driven by a desire to prove how much our teacher or mentor meant to us. We want to show this person that his or her attention and guidance really helped. What is true for you?

9. When you are or were present with this significant person in your life, what do you think about yourself?

   Maybe you suddenly believed that you had an ability you didn't know you had. Or maybe it was a whole new attitude, such as "life really is worth living."

10. When you are or were present with this significant person in your life, how do you feel about yourself?

    State how you feel, for example, "I feel cared for," "I feel special," or "I feel excited and engaged." Make room for how you felt about the relationship then and how you feel about it today.

11. When you are or were present with this significant person in your life, how do you behave toward yourself?

   Are you more nurturing or more judging?

12. How has the way you think, feel, and behave toward yourself around this significant person impacted your life and others' lives?

   Maybe just thinking about this person's influence on your life today can prompt you to act in a more focused, confident manner? Describe how this is true if it fits for you.

This is a life area where you may feel complete with the awareness that you gained by responding to the basic questions. However, it's also possible that an emotion did emerge that is linked to a significant negative core belief. For example, if you declared that this relationship enabled you to think, "I really do have capabilities," this might have sharply contrasted with the view you carried from your parents that "I will never amount to anything." That's a phrase that certainly can be worthwhile for you to track now to see what memories and attitudes are behind it. Scan your own responses now to determine whether you have a statement that merits further review. If only positive beliefs and emotions show up, then simply move to the next area.

YOUR IN-LAWS

We've all seen those portrayals: the "in-laws from hell." Most are caricatures and greatly exaggerated, of course. And yet, the reality is that many of us do face challenges in forging relationships with our in-laws or trying to avoid having much of a relationship with them at all. We'd like to think that we married our spouse, not our spouse's parents, and we tend not to hold these relationships at nearly the same level of importance as our connection with our own parents. Still, our in-laws do actively enter into our lives, and feelings and frustrations often get stirred. You will have the opportunity to look at how your relationships with your in-laws impact you in this section.

What if you don't have in-laws because you're not married, or because your partner's parents have passed away? Do you get a "pass" here and receive a free ticket to move right along to the next area of life? Not necessarily. You are in charge of your own Awareness Integration journey, so if you really want to simply mark "does not apply" at this stop, you may certainly do so. But I have a different suggestion: Take full advantage of the questions in this area to see what material might emerge by addressing them in a different way.

How? Well, if you're divorced, you did have in-laws in your life at some point. Even if you no longer maintain regular contact with them now, they probably still left an impact on you. If you considered marriage or a lifetime commitment with a potential spouse or partner, you most likely met your prospective in-laws—or heard a whole lot about them. And even if you've never had a set of in-laws show up in the picture of your life, you can go through the steps in this section with an imagined sense of having in-laws. You may have predetermined ideas of how you would relate to them, and how they would relate to you. This could be very useful information in your growing awareness. Give it a try.

FERNANDO AND MARIA

I was once assisting a couple, Fernando and Maria, who had very different styles of communication. Those differences flared up when they brought each other's parents into the marital equation. Fernando spoke in a raw, direct, no-nonsense manner. Maria, in contrast, was a sweet talker who preferred to include a lot of "fluff" in whatever she was going to say. Each partner had learned their behavior from their parents, so it was natural that the sharp contrast showed up in communication with their in-laws.

Here's how it all came to a head: Maria and Fernando clashed over financial issues, especially as it related to loans that Maria had taken out and needed to repay. Fernando's mother heard about this from her son and spoke her piece to Maria, in the same raw and direct family style. Maria was stung. Did her mother-in-law not love her? The mother-in-law stirred up the pot even more by blurting out her opinion to Maria's parents, who were shocked at what seemed to them to be rudeness.

The way out of this in-law mess was for both Fernando and Maria to learn and accept why their in-laws behaved as they did. Maria needed to see that cultural influences shaped the manner in which her husband and his parents communicated. Fernando needed to see that in order to have a harmonious relationship with his in-laws, he would have to treat them differently than he treated his own parents. Each partner worked with his or her emotions, and after releasing the "charge" around them, they were able to take steps toward moving in those new and more helpful directions.

For those who do have in-laws, it may be helpful to consider how your relationship with them is colored by your relationship with your parents. Many clients who have taken the Awareness Integration journey notice that if they look at their own parents as basically good and loving, they are more likely to accept their in-laws and assume they will be similar. But those whose parents were not so good and loving often project that perspective onto their in-laws and create a critical view of them. Sometimes, however, if we struggled with our own parents but seem to have an easier time relating to our in-laws, we rush to a posture of idolizing them as the positive opposite of our parents. Take a look at your own situation.

Our relationships with our in-laws are also shaped by the relationship our spouse has to them as his or her own parents. If your spouse tends to be defensive toward his or her parents, it may hold you back from saying anything that could be construed as remotely critical of your in-laws, out of deference to your spouse. You can't say "I can't stand your dad" in the same way you might openly say that about your own father. It's quite possible that you have needed to work hard to learn boundaries in your relationship with your in-laws to avoid creating further problems for your spouse. Or maybe you've gotten caught right in the middle of your spouse's battles with his or her parents.

As always, there are no right or wrong answers here. You're simply taking inventory of your particular thoughts, feelings, and behavior so that you can cultivate greater awareness, release emotions that distort your way of being, and claim new and more workable attitudes and identities. Let's see how that might work for you in this area of life.

1. What do you think of your in-laws?

   You can also explore your thoughts about your spouse's relationship to his or her family with this question too.

2. How do you feel about your in-laws?

   Write both positive/pleasurable and negative/uncomfortable emotions. These may be feelings that you have shared with your in-laws directly, or with your spouse, but they may also be feelings that you have chosen not to share. If so, note your attitude toward making this choice.

3. How do you behave toward your in-laws?

   Does your spouse look at your behavior toward his or her parents the same or differently as you would describe your behavior toward them? Is there any friction between you and your spouse because of how you act toward your in-laws, or have you instead bonded more deeply because of a common sense for how you will both relate to them? Another way to examine this question is to include how you would like to behave toward your in-laws if you didn't have to worry about your spouse's reaction.

4. How does the way you think, feel, and behave toward your in-laws impact your life and others' lives?

   You may find that the impact is significant, or you may simply observe that you have managed to keep this relationship in a very different context than your relationship with your parents. It may not affect you much one way or another.

5. When your in-laws are around you, what do you assume they think about you?

   They may be very direct in displaying their attitude toward you, or they may be more guarded. Either way, you probably have some idea of what they think of you.

6. When your in-laws are around you, how do you assume they feel about you?

   Do they seem happy to be around you, or are they anxious when in your presence? If your in-laws seem frustrated or angry with you or say critical things of you, how does your spouse respond?

7. When your in-laws are around you, how do you experience their behavior toward you?

   Do they fully engage with you when you get together, or do they keep their distance? Do they sometimes treat you as an appendage to their son or daughter rather than as a real person? Do their actions ever get in the way of your relationship with your spouse?

8. How has the way that you assume your in-laws think, feel, and behave toward you when they are around you impacted your life and others' lives?

   You may notice that whether your in-laws have a high or not-so-high regard for you, it doesn't really faze you. Then again, it may affect you very deeply. Give voice to that reality for yourself here.

9. When you are present with your in-laws, what do you think about yourself?

   Do you give yourself a pat on the back because you keep proper boundaries and act with genuine respect? Or is there a different attitude toward yourself that emerges? "I am the best," "I am not patient enough," or "They are lucky to have me."

10. When you are present with your in-laws, how do you feel about yourself?

    Write your positive and negative emotions. Notice how your feelings about yourself in relation to your in-laws may be connected to your feelings about yourself related to your parents. You may find yourself saying, "Thank God these are not my parents" or, on the flip side, "I wish my parents were more like them." What feelings toward yourself are lurking behind these assessments or judgments? Anger that you're not speaking up, sadness that you are not a priority, or shame because you think they like their other son- or daughter-in-law more than you?

11. When you are present with your in-laws, how do you behave toward yourself?

    If you find yourself tip-toeing around your in-laws, do you get down on yourself for becoming "small"? Do you retreat from contact with them to avoid your anxiety in their presence, only to find yourself feeling even worse for being so avoidant?

12. How does the way that you think, feel, and behave about yourself when you are around your in-laws impact your life and others' lives?

    Look for any way that your relationship with your in-laws has helped you gain perspective on how you deal with your own parents. Maybe there is a door opening to new behavior on that front?

Now it's your turn to explore any charge you have felt in responding to the questions in this life area. That charge can help you open the door to explore and release your strongest core negative belief. Go to appendix A for the complete exercise.

Chapter Five

Love, Romance, and All the By-products

Sweet, and yet bitter at times, is romance, the chocolate of our life. The area of intimate relationships begins from teen years and continues to be one we deal with for a lifetime. You can begin with the past relationships to become more aware of your patterns in choosing a mate and behaving in an intimate relationship, and then explore the relationship that you're in now. There is also an opportunity to explore your ideas, emotions, and behaviors toward sex. And then we go to the fruits of your love, your children.

YOUR PAST INTIMATE/ROMANTIC RELATIONSHIPS

For better or for worse, all of our intimate or romantic relationships leave their footprints on us. We make decisions in our new relationships based in large part on the pleasure or the heartbreak we encountered when we got close to somebody else in the past.

Often this takes the form of a knee-jerk reaction. If, for example, we conclude that the problem with our past relationship was that he was an introvert, we figure that we just need to find an extrovert and all shall be well. When this new relationship goes sour, we get either lost or confused, gun-shy from seeking new relationship partners, or we make a new declaration, such as, "She was too pushy so I'll just find a woman who goes with the flow." And we wind up caught in a pattern that keeps re-creating itself.

That's why taking the time to bring awareness to our past relationships is so vital and beneficial. We can begin to unlock the door to understanding how we think, feel, and behave in our relationships, and how our manner of approaching relationships may be blocking our way to a fulfilling connection with someone we love.

So you're going to trace your relationship history. I invite you to begin with your first important relationship, which may or may not be the first person you dated or even the first person with whom you shared sexual intimacy. We're looking for the first time you believed you had truly fallen in love. Beginning with that relationship, consider your part in it. I know, it's all too easy to focus our relationship anger or frustration on what we didn't like about the other person, but the goal here is to gain awareness of your own way of being in a relationship. That is what will inform your choices in the healthiest way going forward.

If you have never been in an intimate relationship, go over the questions and explore what had stopped you. What were the obstacles that held you from choosing, entering, or maintaining an intimate relationship?

As you explore that first relationship and then the next ones, consider first what you had learned about relationships from others. Did you regard your parents' relationship as a model, or did you listen to messages from the culture, religion, friends, or some romantic movie or book that caught your fancy? Did you enter into those early relationships because you felt you had to due to peer pressure or your age at the time, or was it really a conscious choice? What was the attraction—purely physical or more emotional? What meaning did you give to the relationship? Were you swept up in the belief that this "perfect love" would make everything about your life neat and pretty?

What was happening when the relationship began to fizzle? Did you get shy and not give in to love? Did you turn controlling or demanding? Did you turn a blind eye to obvious signs that you didn't belong in this relationship but trudge forward anyway? Did you initiate the breakup, or did your partner? Did you project that your partner was rejecting you when you actually had been indirectly rejecting your partner for quite some time?

Take a few moments brainstorming some of these ideas before you dive into the Awareness Integration core questions. You won't have all the answers after this simple brainstorming, but you will get a good start, so that the questions ahead will yield greater insights and more productive conclusions about your attitudes and beliefs, and what you might do about them.

Are you ready to take inventory of your past relationships, and to gently shine the spotlight on you rather than the others? Answering the questions that follow will help you take the first steps to learn what you have brought with you into the current relationship.

1. What do you think of your past romantic partner or intimate relationships?
   You can survey your attitude toward all your relationships in general, but it may be more productive to look at each one individually. If you

find yourself launching into blame of your partners, simply become aware that this is your first impulse. Then see what else you think about those relationships, from a wider lens.

2. How do you feel about your past romantic partner or intimate relationships?

 Do you feel love, adoration, or safety? Or perhaps you are angry at how you were treated or how things didn't work out. Write both positive/pleasurable and negative/uncomfortable emotions. Might there also be sadness in there, or perhaps a yearning to return to a simpler time of being in relationships?

3. How do you behave toward your past romantic partner or intimate relationships?

 Write both actions/behaviors that have created favorable results and ones that have created unfavorable results. Do you still keep in contact, or is it done and over with? Do you love to tell your friends all the juicy or sordid details, or do you keep your thoughts and feelings private? If so, are you ashamed or embarrassed, trying to protect an identity?

4. How does the way you think, feel, and behave toward your past romantic partner or intimate relationships impact your life, his or her life, or your current partner's life?

 It's very likely that it has impacted your more recent relationships. But look beyond that direct connection and see where else your attitude about your relationship history enters into your life. Perhaps a fear of intimacy has extended into fear in other life domains.

5. When your past relationship partners were around you, what do you assume they thought about you?

 Most likely they spoke up about what they thought of you, and that attitude or judgment certainly left its mark. But did you sometimes wonder if they were thinking something different about you than what they shared? Feel free to include those thoughts.

6. When your past relationship partners were around you, how do you assume they felt about you?

 You may be hearing the echoes from the arguments or battles you had together, but you may again want to widen the lens. How do you imagine they felt about you in happier or more peaceful times?

7. When your past relationship partners were around you, how did you experience their behavior toward you?

 It may help to break down those past relationships into phases or periods: How did a particular partner behave toward you in the beginning, in the middle, and toward the end?

ELAINE'S STORY

Elaine was tracking her five previous relationships, and she soon got excited about detecting a very clear, consistent timeline that each one seemed to follow. The first six months were nothing but passion and love. For the next six months she would pick and nag about whatever was wrong with the guy, and she could always find something to nag about. From the one-year mark until the two-year mark, she would try to change him. At the two-year mark, she became resigned to not being able to change him. On the two-and-a-half-year mark, she dumped him and then filled out a detailed list of what was wrong with him.

That was valuable awareness, but where did it come from? When Elaine closed her eyes, she immediately saw herself with her mother. As she discovered, her pattern with men related directly to how her mom had treated her dad, except that she never dumped him. She just kept nagging him, which created a dark cloud that Elaine had to survive under. From the pain she suffered, Elaine wound up unconsciously repeating her mother's relationship pattern with a twist of hoping for a better one to come around so that she would not feel stuck like her mother.

"You could have been with a prince, and you would still pick his behavior apart," I pointed out. "You're right, I never gave those guys a chance," she sighed. This realization, combined with a release of the sadness from witnessing her mother's way of being with her father, set her free. She went on to forge a healthy relationship that made it past the two-year mark! They were able to take steps toward moving in those new and more helpful directions.

8. How has the way you assume your past relationship partners thought, felt, and behaved toward you impacted your life, his or her life, and your current partner's life?

    We have already looked at knee-jerk reactions. If my partner believed I was too fat, did I believe that I just needed to lose thirty pounds and then anyone would love me and never want to leave me? If you reacted in similar ways, how well did this response serve you?

9. When you consider your past romantic or intimate relationships, what do you think about yourself?

Do you see yourself as having been naïve and foolish? Or can you validate your willingness to be in relationships and appreciate that they may have at least temporarily helped you see yourself as lovable?

Notice statements that may arise here that reflect a negative core belief: "Relationships are not worth the aggravation!" or "I'm never going to be that vulnerable again!" or "Why did I keep picking such jerks?" There are feelings behind those statements that you can track in a moment.

10. When you consider your past romantic or intimate relationships, how do you feel about yourself?

    Do you feel proud, lovable, and cared for, or do you feel shamed, betrayed, sad, and so forth? How do you feel about yourself and your behavior?

11. When you consider your past romantic or intimate relationships, how do you behave toward yourself?

    Do you shake your head in disgust for allowing yourself to be hurt? Or do you nod in understanding that you did the best you could and that your job now is to learn from what happened?

12. How does the way that you think, feel, and behave toward yourself when considering your past romantic partner or intimate relationships impact your life, his or her life, and your current partner's life?

    Maybe this reflection on your past relationships makes you want to write a book about it? Be my guest! It is very important for you to see the impact on your current relationship.

So take a look at what patterns you see in your relationship history from the previous questions and the core beliefs you attach to your attitudes about what happened. Let's examine more closely what's behind them. Go to appendix A for the complete exercise.

YOUR CURRENT INTIMATE/ROMANTIC RELATIONSHIP

Your current romantic or intimate relationship is probably the most intimate and impactful connection you have, other than your relationship with your parents. Its influence extends into almost every other domain of your life. Your ability to gain a deeper awareness of your current relationship can be a key factor in creating the change you wish to see in your life. If one of your major goals in following the Awareness Integration journey is to seek greater fulfillment in your life, this is one of the most pivotal areas that can help make that happen. When you truly learn about who you are in your relationship, that understanding can serve as a bridge toward healing childhood traumas. When that healing happens, you bear the fruit in all realms of life.

Just think for a moment about the influence of your relationship on your life. If your relationship is solid and satisfying, chances are very good that other parts of your life are also apt to be more successful and fulfilling. But if your relationship is not working, everything in your life may suffer: work or career, social life, spiritual connection, and so forth.

I have seen with clients I work with and others I know that if we are fulfilled in our relationship but struggle with some other realm, such as our job, that job frustration won't be as difficult to absorb. It just has a different feel to it because we have that foundation of a positive relationship at home as a buffer. On the flip side, let's say you do have success in your career but your relationships, including the one you're in, have been a constant source of pain and frustration. You say to yourself, "I work hard, but for what? Is work the sole reason for my existence?" So even as you are fulfilled in your work, you may feel alone or empty inside.

It's critical, then, to become aware of your belief systems shaping your current relationship. And if you don't have a relationship, you can explore what belief systems may be sabotaging you in your efforts to attract a satisfying union. When you looked back at your relationship history in the last stop on the Awareness Integration trail, you gained awareness of what attitudes or beliefs have contributed negatively to past relationships. The question now becomes, are you still living by that same attitude in your relationship today? Are you still guided by fantasies, rather than seeing with the eyes of reality? Do you still act defensively or protect yourself with your intimate partner because of past heartbreak?

In general, how are your beliefs and attitudes about your relationship working or not working for you? When you go through the questions of the model and apply them to this area, be on the lookout for how your beliefs are creating what's happening in the here and now. That's so much of what this work is all about! If you do recognize how your beliefs are creating your experience, then you have no need to project what's happening onto your partner. You can take responsibility for what you are creating within your relationship.

There are many other questions to consider as you prepare for this part of the journey. How do you express love? Do you express it verbally, physically, through buying things, or by doing favors? What do you want or expect in terms of how love is expressed to you? How do you define power in your relationship and who wields it? Sometimes we think our relationship is all about being equals, but a closer look reveals that one or both of us is trying to gain control by acting righteous or being manipulative. Or perhaps you share power, so you assume power over money matters and sex but your partner has control over your social life and childrearing.

What do you do together? How do you play together? How do you fight, and what are the rules? Is it about winning or understanding each other? How do you resolve differences and conflict, or do you avoid conflict at all costs? What roles might each of you be playing: Is one of you the parent and the other the child? Is the parent figure a scolding parent or a nurturing parent? How is your behavior toward your mate colored by the example of how your parents related to one another? That's a subject we will focus on in greater detail in the next life area.

Remember, even if you do not have a current relationship, there is much material you can uncover here.

DANIEL'S STORY (PART 1)

When my young client Daniel reached this point of the model, he came to grips with his sadness about never having had an intimate relationship with a woman. In exploring his attitudes and beliefs about that, he discovered a duality: One part of him was self-confident, and another part of him was very insecure. That insecure part was holding him back from approaching young women to become close enough to explore relationship possibilities.

In bridging that duality, Daniel soon came in contact with an "alpha male part" that he could call upon when being around women. He also needed skill building to practice how to speak up, to share more of himself, to carry a conversation forward, to show authentic interest in the other person's life, and to feel at ease engaging in physical contact. We worked on the development of these skills at this stop of his journey, and again when we revisited this life area on phase two of his Awareness Integration process. That's something you will be able to do as well. Before long, Daniel was reporting significant progress in the "laboratory," which for him meant being around women at school.

"I feel a little more confident around them, a little less self-conscious," he said. "I feel like most of them are like me, you know? And it seems like they turn their heads my way now whenever they're walking by me."

So even though Daniel did not manifest the relationship of his dreams right away, he felt more comfortable and confident and could see the light shining on the path ahead.

Now it's your turn to shine the light on your current relationship path. May the magic of Awareness Integration point you in the direction you need to go.

1. What do you think of your current romantic partner or intimate relationship?

    Write both positive and negative thoughts. Notice right away that this question, like the others that will follow, does not just ask what you think of your relationship partner. It also asks what you think of your relationship as a living entity in your life. One consideration may be what kind of expectation you have about this relationship: Is it apt to endure, or are you simply exploring?

2. How do you feel about your current romantic partner or intimate relationship?

    Write both positive/pleasurable and negative/uncomfortable emotions. It's important to give voice to what feelings you share with your mate and, if applicable, what feelings you conceal. This is your opportunity to look at your own feelings in a safe way.

3. How do you behave toward your current romantic partner or intimate relationship?

    Your answer will naturally include how you actually behave toward your relationship partner in day-to-day life. But it can also cover your inward behavior toward your relationship: Do you give yourself fully to it or hold yourself back?

4. How does the way you think, feel, and behave toward your current romantic partner or intimate relationship impact your life and his or her life?

    As we discussed earlier in this section, it's quite likely that your attitude toward your relationship is influencing your work, your friendships, and much of your whole life. Take a broad inventory of what that influence looks like for you.

    This is also a great place to take full responsibility for the way you impact not only your relationship with your partner but also his or her life in totality.

5. When your partner is around you, what do you assume he or she thinks about you?

    Does your partner regard you with respect or with frequent disapproval? Does your partner ignore you or engage you? Is there equality? How well do you think this person really knows you?

6. When your partner is around you, what do you assume he or she feels about you?

    This may incorporate feelings that are expressed to you directly, or feelings that you sense your partner is experiencing but keeps a lid on, at least until those emotions spill out in covert or passive-aggressive ways.

7. When your partner is around you, how do you experience his or her behavior toward you?

If you really love and appreciate how your mate treats you, now is the time to fully acknowledge and celebrate that! Sometimes we get so caught up in occasional conflicts that we fail to see the big picture of how well our

MELISSA AND JEFFREY'S STORY

Melissa and Jeffrey had been married more than twenty years when they came to see me, and I applied this area of the Awareness Integration Model to address their challenges. Jeffrey was an addict, though mostly functional in his life. Melissa played a mostly passive role in the relationship, though her behavior turned more passive aggressive in allowing her anger about his addiction to seep through. He had recently taken an important step by entering rehab, but the healthier he became, the more her rage intensified. Why? As we explored the questions related to the model, Melissa gained awareness of her responsibility: She had become accustomed to not saying directly what she needed to say and then provoking him with her behavior. With the addiction temporarily offstage, her pent-up anger about what had been happening all that time prior to his rehab came storming out.

Awareness was the first part of creating a change. Then we needed to track her feelings of anger. Not surprisingly, Melissa learned that she was acting just like her mom had acted with her dad: passivity followed by indirect expressions of anger. "You see, you were following a pattern unconsciously," I pointed out. Once she understood this, she was free to pursue a new course. Healing the mother inside her allowed her rage to subside, and learning new communication skills enabled her to speak her mind. When Jeffrey relapsed, she set firm boundaries. She understood that his addiction and recovery were his responsibility. If he stayed clean, she would be there for him. If not, she felt confident that she could end the relationship. She had become one strong woman, a powerful example of how, when you let go of fear, you can be authentically loving.

And what about those positive influences in the rest of Melissa's life? She had never worked, but now, at the age of forty-one, she went back to nursing school to help support herself, and her husband. She just felt more on top of her life and the world around her. As for Jeffrey, he was strong enough to return to therapy. His relapse lasted a much shorter period of time than earlier relapses, and he was soon devoted to his recovery program again. Having a much more solid marriage was a major source of support for him on that front.

mate really does treat us. However, if you know that you are being treated badly, take an honest look at that here, and consider what steps you need to take to address the situation.

8. How has the way that you assume your partner thinks, feels, and behaves toward you impacted your life and his or her life?

    If you sense that you are truly loved and respected, it may provide you with an enormous boost in self-confidence. If so, what is the value of that contribution? If the relationship is in turmoil, and you feel judged or misunderstood, how is that working against you on the larger stage of life?

9. When you are present with your current relationship partner, what do you think about yourself?

    You might say, "I'm pretty darned lucky to have this relationship" or, "It depends what day you ask the question." Flesh out what you mean so it becomes useful to you in your awareness.

10. When you are present with your current relationship partner, how do you feel about yourself?

    Do you feel like a king or queen? Do you feel anxious, as if you're walking on eggshells? Are you invisible? Do you feel significant? Explore these feelings.

11. When you are present with your current relationship partner, how do you behave toward yourself?

    Are you being your full self, or are you holding yourself back? Are you comfortable?

12. How does the way that you think, feel, and behave toward yourself when you are around your current relationship partner impact your life and his or her life?

    This is where you need to pay attention to what is really going on inside. There may be something about your relationship that is impacting your inner life, not just your day-to-day contact with your mate. Is something that you feel about yourself in this relationship making you doubt yourself in totality? What is going on there, and how is that affecting you?

If you are married, do not feel concerned if you happen to be pursuing this Awareness Integration journey solo. The work that you do now in releasing emotions and adopting new attitudes and beliefs will certainly pay dividends in your relationship. Find your starting point from the responses you have generated so far by looking for those places where you felt a strong emotion that is likely pointing you toward a negative core belief.

As you come up with a negative core belief with an emotional charge, go to appendix A for the complete exercise.

If you are married, part of your lab work may be to appropriately share your experience with your spouse. If you need help, perhaps it is time to enlist the aid of a relationship counselor or therapist.

Before we move onto the next life area, I'd like to invite those of you who are married or who are in a committed relationship to consider one more question:

Have you ever had an affair? Have you been the partner who has extended yourself to engage in an extramarital affair? Or are you the lover of someone who is married or in a committed intimate relation?

Be honest with yourself. Remember that you are on this journey for your own growth. If you have participated in one or more extramarital affairs, you can

MARRY AND TOM'S STORY

Marry and Tom told me that their relationship had begun with excitement and optimism, that they got along great but that recently Tom had expressed reservations about being ready for marriage and Marry was backing away more herself. When I guided Marry into tracing her past relationships, she revealed that this was only her second intimate connection. "I found out that the first guy had been lying and cheating on me for months," she revealed. Feeling hurt and betrayed, she concluded, "I can't trust anyone." So with her current boyfriend, she had begun to play detective, looking for the evidence of his betrayal that she just knew had to be there. Marry came up blank, and Tom was turned off by her distrust.

As Marry became aware of this dynamic, she recognized that while she certainly didn't want to hide her head in the sand around the behavior of any man in her life again, she also needed to learn how to be loving and to accept when her partner was acting in a way that she could rely and depend on. She needed to learn to trust him and, just as important, to trust herself and her ability to make healthy choices at every step of the relationship path.

While working with Tom who expressed frustration at not finding the woman of his dreams, an examination of his past relationships revealed a pattern in which he was only attracted to "bad-ass girls" whom he would never marry. With awareness of this tendency, he began to see that he needed to learn how to create desire for a woman he actually loved and respected.

take a major step in learning and potentially healing from that experience by responding to the core questions related to that experience right now. So, if this area applies to you, follow the trail of those questions below. If you have never had an affair, you may choose to skip this section. However, you might benefit from looking over the questions anyway, either to reinforce the choices that you have made in steering clear of extramarital affairs or to explore the possible implications if this is a choice you should consider at some point down the road.

1. What do you think of your extramarital affair?

   The most useful answers here, as with any response to the core questions of Awareness Integration, are those that are real and true for you, not what you believe is called for. If "I think it was totally benign" is your truthful thought here, that's what you want to record. Or if your thought is "It was the biggest mistake of my life," then that is what fits for you. Take the time to tune into all your actual thoughts, feelings, and beliefs as these questions continue to unfold here.

2. How do you feel about your extramarital affair?

   Perhaps you would say, "I feel ashamed," "I feel accepting," or "I feel empowered." Simply note your own feelings.

3. How do you behave toward your extramarital affair?

   Do you want to stomp it out of your memory, or do you regard it as a necessary step toward independence? Is it something in between, or totally different?

4. How does the way you think, feel, and behave toward your extramarital affair impact your life, your partner's life, and the life of the person you are having an affair with?

   Has an affair led to a breakup of a relationship? Did it destroy trust? Or did it open a door to looking at the real relationship problems being ignored? If you are having an affair today, how does living with this secret impact you right now, and how do you believe your partner would be impacted if the truth came out?

5. When you imagine others looking at you in regard to his affair, what do you assume they think about you?

   Consider possible judgments or even a nod of understanding. After all, the percentage of married men and women who have affairs is extremely high, right?

6. When you imagine others looking at you in regard to this affair, what do you assume they feel about you?

   It may help to have in mind one or more specific persons in assessing feelings about you here, whether they happen to be family members, friends, religious officials, or someone else.

7. When you imagine others looking at you in regard to this affair, how do you assume they behave toward you?

    Are you shunned or accepted? Do other people seem to want to know all about it, or do they not want to hear about it at all?

8. How has the way that you assume others think, feel, and behave toward you in regard to this affair impacted your life and your partner's life?

    If you have openly dealt with the affair and your relationship is intact, do you still struggle to deal with the judgments of other people?

9. When you were (are) present with your extramarital affair partner, what did/do you think about yourself?

    Again, stick to your truthful responses. For some this might be "I'm bad" or "I'm going to pay for this," but for others it may be "I'm finally doing something for me" or "It was just sex."

10. When you were (are) present with your extramarital affair partner, how did/do you feel about yourself?

    Was guilt your dominant emotion? Was it something else, such as a sense of really being alive for the first time?

11. When you were (are) present with your extramarital affair partner, how did/do you behave toward yourself?

    The behavior may not prominently reveal itself until you are alone again. Note what may have been different in your behavior from before you began the affair.

12. How does the way you think, feel, and behave toward yourself when you are present with your extramarital affair partner impact your life and the lives of the other people involved?

    Those other people include, at the very least, your spouse or current partner, the person with whom you had the affair, that other person's spouse, and your own children. That's a pretty big picture to bring into focus. Your willingness to keep looking at that picture from every angle will certainly help you zero in on what you most need to explore in this realm.

Finally, follow the same process for tracking and releasing your emotions in regard to your affair that you have been using throughout your Awareness Integration journey and welcome any shift or deeper awareness that may emerge. Go to appendix A for the complete exercise.

SEX

Do you talk about sex very much in your life? No, let me amend that question: Do you ever talk about sex in a real way? Many of us often joke about sex but seldom take an honest, open look into the nature of our relationship with our own sexuality and how that impacts our life. That's natural, but in this part of the Awareness Integration journey, you can have an experience of taking that closer look. And if you have been shy about talking about sex, you can safely explore your own feelings now in your private and confidential experience.

What kinds of material might emerge as you respond to the core questions at this stop on the Awareness Integration trail? You may find yourself bringing into your field of awareness the influences on your sexual attitudes and beliefs. Did your views about sex come from your family, your religion, or the culture? Which ones stuck? Even if you acted in rebellion against one or more of those beliefs, is it possible that your behavior was still limited by those views? Maybe you rebelled against a cultural message that premarital sex was wrong, but you felt shame for crossing that boundary.

Let's consider shame for a moment with a wider lens. In my experience in working with clients, I have found that most of us do hold at least a degree of shame related to sex. Either we did something or something was done to us to stir that feeling. It's simply a reality that most of us have had an experience where some inappropriate boundary was crossed, even if that was simply beginning to masturbate when we believed at the time that masturbation was somehow wrong. The shame may also extend to same-gender sex or the desire for it, at a period in life when we lacked our own understanding or conviction that being gay, lesbian, or transgender is totally natural and completely worthy to be embraced as one form of sexual expression. Maybe we also felt shame for simply wanting or practicing some particular fetish. Or we had one moment in childhood where we walked in on our parents having sex or our children walked in on us as adults. Allow yourself to connect with any shameful feelings, knowing you are certainly not alone.

Other areas to explore here include examining what is important to you regarding sex. Is sex mostly for pleasure and excitement? Or is it a need to experience real intimacy with your partner, to share on an emotional as well as a physical level? If you say "that depends," what does it depend on? Do you prefer to give or to receive? Do you engage in sex for validation of being attractive or being a desirable person, or do you regard sex as a confirmation of trust and closeness?

Take a look at how you communicate about sex, or whether you even communicate about it at all with your partners. Do you know your own body and what makes you feel good, and do you take responsibility for getting "hot" and achieving orgasm or other forms of sexual satisfaction? Or do you passively wait for your partner to figure you out and know exactly what to do to press all the right buttons?

I once did counseling with a couple where the man's idea of foreplay was to approach her while she was standing in the kitchen and grab her butt. That sure didn't turn her on. She would just get angry, which left him huffing and puffing in frustration, or she would give in against her true wishes. Both parties needed to gain awareness into their behavior and then make new choices in their sexual dance. He needed to understand that she had different needs regarding what would get her truly excited, but she needed to better understand those needs and then communicate to him what they were. Over time, she got to know her body better and then taught him how to excite her. They even took a visit to their local sex shop together, turning the task of initiating changes in their sexual behavior into play.

How do you choose sexual partners, and how consistent is that approach with your values and intentions in your life? Perhaps you're a guy who wants a "hot mama" for sex but is looking for the Madonna virgin type to marry. Or, as a woman, you like the bad boys who favor impulsive acts around sex but then yearn for a reliable family man as a husband. How do you deal with that kind of duality? And when you think about your history with sex, do you feel as if you have had too many partners, or too few? Why?

So, are you ready to take a peek to see what you can learn about you and sex?

1. What do you think of sex?

    Take stock of your general attitude: Is sex a wonderful experience or something that comes with a lot of "stuff" attached to it in your mind? Who influenced your attitude? It's essential that you're honest with yourself.

2. How do you feel about sex?

    Notice any consistencies as well as any inconsistencies. Perhaps you feel excited about the idea of engaging in sex but then anxious or sad in the experience itself. Or do your feelings depend on the other person and the situation?

3. How do you behave toward sex?

    Write both actions/behaviors that have created favorable results and ones that have created unfavorable results. Are you still like the hormone-raging adolescent, or do your approach sex in a slower, more refined way? What is your sexual style and approach? Do you take on a different persona in bed?

4. How does the way you think, feel, and behave toward sex impact your life and others' lives?

    For some people, having a healthy and active sex life, steered by a positive attitude, is a foundation for a generally satisfying life. For others, the opposite is true. See what may be the case for you. This is your chance to gain awareness about who you really are as a sexual being.

The next series of questions present a challenge since sex is not a person. I leave it to you to experiment with rephrasing the questions to make them meaningful for you. My wording is simply one suggestion.

5. What do you assume your partner or people around you thinks about you and your relationship to sex?

   The people you have in mind here may be sexual partners, or they may be family and friends who simply have some thoughts or ideas about how you seem to relate to sex. Do they think you're too hesitant around sex or too promiscuous? What else may be useful for you to bring to light?

6. How do you assume your partner or people around you feel about you regarding your relationship to sex?

   They may feel sad, happy, or envious about their perception of you and sex. Just note those feelings and witness your response to writing them down or speaking them. If you happen to be gay or lesbian, you may have very strong beliefs about what others feel about you. Give voice to that sense here.

7. How does your partner or people around you behave toward you regarding your relationship with sex?

   Maybe you have received advice, wanted or unwanted. What was said, and how did you receive it?

8. How does the way you assume your partner or people you know think, feel, and behave toward you regarding your relationship with sex impact your life and others' lives?

   One way to extend this inquiry is to think about what the culture may think or feel about your sexual ways. How are you influenced by what the culture would say about your approach to your own sexuality, whether you happen to be heterosexual, gay, lesbian, or transgender?

9. When you are present with your sexuality, what do you think about yourself?

   Write your positive and negative thoughts. Remember that masturbation is a sexual act, so you may want to consider your thoughts when you engage in (or refrain from) that activity.

10. When you are present with your sexuality, how do you feel about yourself?

    Often those feelings are especially intense because of the vulnerability we experience in sex. Reflect on what may be a myriad of feelings that you have ever experienced during sex.

11. When you are present with your sexuality, how do you behave toward yourself?

    Write your positive and negative behavior. Perhaps that behavior does not surface until the immediate aftermath of engaging in a sexual act. What comes up for you right after the heat of the action? Do you judge or blame yourself, or are you filled with a sense of oneness that you want to share with the world?

12. How does the way that you think, feel, and behave toward yourself around your sexuality impact your life and others' lives?

Take the opportunity to consider this impact as it has evolved from preado-
lescence to teenage years, young adulthood, and today. Childhood trauma
regarding sex often surfaces with clients when working in this life area. Some
report that when they begin to get sexually aroused, sadness emerges, which
prompts them to move away from the other person and the experience. That's
the molestation or other trauma showing itself.

Whether your emotions stirred up responding to these questions are linked
to a trauma or not, allow yourself an opportunity to be present with those
feelings, to release them, and to witness a possible opening for healing and
change. If your emotional wounds are deep, it may be time to call upon a
therapist experienced with sexual trauma to help you.

SEXUAL TRAUMA

I had a male client who had ceased having any sexual activity with his wife
because of this issue. He would get sad every time sexual intimacy was in
the air. As he tracked his feelings, he vividly recalled being molested by a
male cousin, someone whom he had loved and trusted. After he got married, he felt the same kind of love for his wife he felt for this cousin. That's
what triggered his sadness and withdrawal. As he allowed this sadness
associated with this memory to wash over him, he experienced a release.

After our continued work, he was able to slowly heal this wounded
part. "That was then and this is now," I advised him. "Today you love
someone whom you can trust not to hurt you."

It took time, of course, but gradually he had the experience of replacing his shame and blame with joy and love.

A female client similarly fell into deep sadness when her husband
approached her sexually. She had clear memories of being molested
by a male neighbor. She had the courage to tell her family about this
inappropriate behavior, but rather than support her they said, "Do not
talk about this!"

She cried and cried in reexperiencing this memory, and that release,
along with the awareness that she gained about her experience, opened
the door to healthy change. As her healing slowly took hold, she was able
to adopt a more welcoming attitude toward sex with her husband. "When
we get close physically now, I can finally remind myself that he is not
that man who hurt me," she said. With this more receptive attitude, she
then turned her attention to building new skills around sex, which for her
meant learning how to have an orgasm. Sex became an act of pleasure.

So, identify those charged feelings, and the negative core beliefs behind them, that you would like to further explore now. Go to appendix A for the complete exercise.

After experiencing a release of emotions, notice if you have a new, more positive core belief to replace an existing negative belief about sex. And if you recognize that new skills are needed to actualize desired changes in your sexual being, your lab work period may be a good time to begin to acquire those skills. Then, during phase two of the Awareness Integration journey, you will have a further opportunity to highlight new goals and needed skills in this important domain.

YOUR CHILDREN

Here is another category that will not directly apply to everyone. So how should you approach this life area if you do not have children? Again, I urge you to go ahead and try on the questions anyway because that process will enable you to explore your attitudes, feelings, and preconceptions about being a parent and raising children. The information that you get back will add to your field of awareness about yourself and your life.

You can make the exploration more useful by adjusting some of the basic wording. For example, instead of asking "What do you think of your children?" you can frame the question as "What do you think of the idea of having children?" No matter what your life situation may be, I'll bet you have something to say about that, and it will most likely shed light on your personal ideology about why people have children and why they don't. So give yourself permission to change the wording of any of the questions and see which ones have meaning to you. If some just don't seem to fit at all, it is fine to pass on them.

Now, what can all of you who do happen to be parents do to prepare for your reflections at this stop on the Awareness Integration trail? For starters, it may be helpful to look at how your perspective of parenting your children has changed through the years. If your kids have grown up, do you find it a bit easier now to say, "I think I was a pretty good parent" or at least "I did the best I could?" Often it's more difficult for parents to say that when their kids are still growing up. If you are still actively parenting, do you sometimes hear the voice that says, "I'm not a good parent?" If you do blame yourself for making mistakes that seem to surface through your children's lives, where do you feel you have fallen short: attention, love, or financial resources? Or when things go wrong with your children, do you get defensive and blame your spouse, or just shake your head in wonder at how your own child could possibly "be that way"? It may be helpful to take a closer look at what you can control and what you can't control. If you have made mistakes, this is a good time to try to forgive yourself. Eventually, all our children become adults with their own responsibility for their lives.

If you have two or more children, your feelings probably differ toward each one. Be sure to fully consider your relationship with each child. If that means repeating the full set of questions for each one individually, you can certainly make that choice. Some parents who have followed the Awareness Integration journey report feelings of shame or guilt for being more connected to one child than another. One male client with two sons confided that his temper would flare easily around his oldest son, whom he often criticized, whereas around his young son he simply felt the urge to reach out and hug him. Shedding awareness of his guilt about this unequal treatment helped him begin to calm down about what he was doing, and then slowly integrate changes in his behavior.

You also have the opportunity in this life area to take a closer look at the manner in which you parent your children. What cues or messages do you follow, and where do those messages come from? Are you simply repeating the parenting behavior that you experienced while growing up, without regard to whether it fits your own beliefs and attitudes? What values have you held as the most important when you're dealing with your children? Is it time to change any of those values or add new ones now?

If you have grandchildren, feel free to incorporate your thoughts, feelings, and behavior when you're around them in this section. Perhaps, like many grandparents, you have discovered that pure joy that comes with being able to love young people without the responsibility of parenting them from day to day. But does that freedom also come with new layers of guilt for having your favorite grandchild? You can also extend your exploration here into how you relate to your adult child's spouse. What kind of in-law are you?

Parents who have raised children with special needs may be carrying especially charged feelings about their experiences. But anyone who has faced the challenge of parenting a child has been through "the fire." Be kind to yourself as you take inventory of how you have managed to engage with your children when the heat was rising.

1. What do you think of your children?

Look to balance statements that reflect your thoughts about your children as a group with responses that specifically describe your thoughts related to each individual child. If your thoughts immediately sound harsh, remember that this is simply an exercise in gaining awareness. You are allowing your uncensored thoughts to surface for examination. One thought usually does not tell the whole story. Keep tracking your responses to all of the questions here.

2. How do you feel about your children?

Do you feel pure love, frustration, or sadness? If your children are older, give yourself the freedom to contrast your feelings during their childhood with your feelings today.

3. How do you behave toward your children?

Write both actions/behaviors that have created favorable results and ones that have created unfavorable results. If your children are adults, do you still find yourself wanting to correct them or direct them in the same way you did when they were ten years old? If so, how do you handle that temptation?

If you find yourself needing to rebut one of your children's claims about how you behave toward them with what you believe is true, this is your forum.

4. How does the way you think, feel, and behave toward your children impact your life and others' lives?

I know, this question could spark volumes of material. As you sift through what you might say, listen especially for statements that seem to have an emotional charge associated with them. That's where your core beliefs may be waiting for discovery. You can mark them for follow-up when we move on to the tracking emotions phase of this life area.

5. What do you assume your children think about you?

Try to be true to what you sense is true about how your children regard you. Then, if you need to add a comment about how "it isn't fair," give yourself that chance. You may also notice again a contrast between how your children perceived you when they were young and how they look at you today.

6. How do you assume your children feel about you?

Write your positive and negative assumptions. Your children no doubt have let you know how they feel about you many times. What do they say, and how does it make you feel? Some children hold in their real feelings about their parents. If you believe that may be true with one or more of your children, why do you think this may be so?

7. How do you experience your children's behavior toward you?

I invite you to give equal time to both how they have behaved toward you in a loving manner and the ways they have acted that upset or disappoint you.

8. How has the way that you assume your children think, feel, and behave toward you impacts your life and others' lives?

If you have several children, it can be revealing to consider how the impact of your experiences with your oldest child shaped your parenting style with your younger children.

I'd like to offer a new twist to this part of the exploration. Take a moment to bring thoughts about your spouse into this parenting picture. Ask the first set of questions again related to your spouse: What does your spouse think, feel, and behave toward your children? Then ask how your children think, feel, and behave toward your spouse as the "other" parent.

I'll tell you why I suggest expanding your picture in this way. I was working with Amy who reported deep sadness because "my kids love my husband more than they love me." This perception was reinforced by her husband's judgments that she parented just like her mother. So we explored these questions, and my clients discovered that her kids did indeed like how their father was playful with them. Then she made a more important discovery. As she considered how her children felt and behaved toward her, she could see that they really loved her just as much as they loved their dad, only differently. She wasn't regarded as the playmate but was highly valued as the nurturer. "Wow, they do love me!" she said. "I guess I'm not such a failure."

So look at how your spouse relates to your children, and how your children relate to your spouse, for your own insights and awareness.

9. When you are present with your children, what do you think about yourself?

   Write your positive and negative thoughts. Watch for those judgments, and as I mentioned, try to be gentle while giving voice to what comes up. Notice also whether your thoughts about yourself while in connection with your own kids bring you back to thoughts and attitudes about when you were a child yourself.

10. When you are present with your children, how do you feel about yourself?

    Write your positive and negative emotions. If you feel mostly proud and happy, by all means make room for those positive responses. One of the advantages of asking these questions at each life area is that it encourages you to connect with your feelings in many different contexts. So your feelings are not likely to all line up consistently under one theme. Allow all your different feelings to emerge.

11. When you are present with your children, how do you behave toward yourself?

    Do you need to control yourself constantly so that you are not controlling them, or do you allow yourself to enjoy them just by being around them or doing a task together? Do you still judge yourself for every act of theirs that you don't like? Do you get disappointed for not offering them all that you could have?

12. How does the way that you think, feel, and behave toward yourself around your children impact your life and others' lives?

This response could also cover a wide spectrum of time. You may want to break it down into periods: when your kids were young, when they were growing up, current day, and so forth.

As soon as he began to explore this life area, Sam had a lot to say about his "troubled" child. It seems that his son would often say hurtful things to Sam because "he has a rage inside of him." Sam felt responsible for that rage and experienced deep sadness and grief about how he believed he had failed as a parent. "I wasn't very qualified to have a child," he lamented. When I asked him where he felt that sadness, he didn't hesitate for a second. "In my heart," he said.

So we tracked that sadness in his heart. Soon the intensity of that primary emotion had dissipated a good bit. Just allowing the feelings to have room and giving voice to something that was so deeply ingrained in him was very helpful. Also helpful was his previous experience with twelve-step programs. He remembered the Serenity Prayer: "God, grant me the serenity to accept the things I cannot change, the courage to change the things I can, and the wisdom to know the difference."

Do you have lessons to call upon that will enable your more difficult feelings about your children and you to be released? Find a negative core belief or charged statement from your responses to this life area, and start the tracking process to see how you can facilitate a healthy shift. If you sense that you may have more than one negative core belief at play, start with the one that seems to have the most intensity for you. Go to appendix A for the complete exercise.

Now you have the opportunity to spend the next several days conducting your follow-up detective work on what happens in your interactions with your children. If you are not in regular contact with them, you might want to call upon photos, e-mails, or other evidence to continue to raise your awareness about these important relationships.

Chapter Six

Mom and Dad

So here we are, more than halfway through the various life areas to be covered on your Awareness Integratioan journey, and we are just now coming to visit your parents individually. Of course, you have probably found yourself coming face-to-face with your father and mother once or multiple times in your reflections while responding to questions in other areas, especially in the memories that you looked at while tracking your emotions. We know our parents' influence is central to our being and follows us wherever we go, regardless of our age. I could have brought your father and mother in much earlier on your journey, but I wanted to help provide you with an opportunity to expand your awareness of many different kinds of relationships and life situations first. Now, hopefully, your exploration of these pivotal relationships from childhood will take on an even greater dimension and will yield the kinds of discoveries and shifts that will serve you in all realms of life.

YOUR FATHER

So we begin with your father. I trust that your answers will flow freely and openly once you begin wading through the basic questions for this area of the model, so we'll spend only a couple of moments preparing you for this stop. You certainly may find yourself taking stock of how well you were able to trust your father as a loving, caring figure, or to what degree you distrusted him and why. If he's always been there for you, you no doubt have felt the positive effects of that connection wherever you have journeyed in life. But if you experienced a loss of that trust, accompanied by hurtful behavior, that sting likewise has followed you through the years. You will be able to see more closely how those experiences and perceptions have impacted you.

If you suffered any form of abuse at the hands of your father, someone entrusted with taking care of you, a sense of deep betrayal may dominate your feelings. Being abused by a father or a mother simply breaks our soul. If you have been wounded in this way, I hope you have called upon professional resources to help you heal. Hopefully, your exploration in this area of the model will enable you to take a further step on the path to healing.

Whatever the nature of your relationship with your father has been, it may be helpful to consider how the father-child connection differs for boys and girls. If you are a woman, did your dad smother you with love and affection when you were a little girl? If you are a man, did he treat you differently, showing less affection because you were a boy? It can also be insightful to consider the transition of your relationship with your father when you began to grow up. What happened when you hit puberty and entered adolescence?

For girls, that is a time when a father needs to start disconnecting physically. That same little girl who used to sit on his lap and kiss him on the mouth now has hormones kicking in. If both father and daughter recognize this, they can transition in a healthy way, so that her physical feelings and impulses can be focused on guys beginning to show up in her life. However, if the father backs away too soon or too dramatically, she may feel rejected. And if he tries to hold on to a place where he no longer belongs, she may feel anxious. What was true in your experience?

As boys grow up, Dad usually becomes less of a playmate and the person who disciplines them, and more of a role model. If you're a man, was your father a positive role model, or did you need to look elsewhere for that example and support? Also, did you have to go through a period of fighting against your dad to prove your independence, and if so, what were the lasting effects of that battle? If you approached him with a "you don't know, I know" posture, did that transform into a more peaceful connection, or did the battle lines remain firmly drawn?

Often our thoughts, feelings, and behavior toward our fathers come down to whether we would say we loved him or hated him. Or did he love me or not love me? Or maybe he used to love me but then stopped, leaving a huge hole from the betrayal.

Whether you have a very clear and specific reference point for this father relationship, or whether it tends to shift depending on time and circumstance, I urge you to go through each question openly and honestly.

1. What do you think of your father?

   Begin with your simple perceptions of him as a man, as a person in his own right. Yes, he is and always will be seen through the lens of his role in your life, but can you step back and consider him at least partly as just one human being? What do you think of this person? Would you say "he is a kind, generous man" or "he is selfish and irresponsible."

2. How do you feel about your father?

   Write both positive/pleasurable and negative/uncomfortable emotions, for example, "I can't stand him"; "I wish he didn't leave our family"; "I really miss him"; or "I'm so grateful he was my Dad." What voice is waiting to be heard to capture your feelings?

3. How do you behave toward your father?

   How did you act toward him as a child, and how do you act toward him, or his memory, today? Or do you do whatever you can to show your love and care, especially if you sense you may not have much time left with him?

4. How does the way you think, feel, and behave toward your father impact your life and others' lives?

   Sometimes as adults, we find there are things that can't be resolved directly with our father and so we simply allow the issues to be what they are. Still, there may be residue that does affect us. Take a look at your own situation.

5. What do you assume your father thinks about you?

   Write your positive and negative assumptions. What do you assume he thought about you when you were a child, a teen, and now as an adult?

6. How do you assume your father feels about you?

   From the long-ago past through today, have his feelings toward you remained consistent? Or have they changed?

7. How does your father behave toward you?

   For some fathers, how they act toward us may be different when they are alone with us as opposed to being with us while in the company of our mother. When you spend time just with him, how does he behave?

8. How has the way that you assume your father thinks, feels, and behaves toward you impacted your life and others' lives?

   Have you had to deal with his disapproval, and if so have you been able to stop seeking that approval? Or has he been supportive and understanding of you as you are, and if so how has that helped you?

9. In your father's presence, what do you think about yourself?

   Write your positive and negative thoughts. Many clients say things such as "I think I'm never going to be good enough"; "I don't think I can make him love me"; or "I know I am always loved and supported."

10. In your father's presence, how do you feel about yourself?

    Do you feel small or inadequate? Do you feel proud because you have fulfilled his dream?

11. In your father's presence, how do you behave toward yourself?

    Do you monitor every word and facial expression, careful not to push his buttons? Or do you let loose safely with who you are with whatever expression you have?

12. How does the way that you think, feel, and behave when you are present with your father impact your life and others' lives?

    This is a question where it may be appropriate to look at the past. What is the carry-over, positive or negative, from the way that you felt in his presence as a child?

FARA'S STORY (PART 2)

When Fara worked on this area of the model, her feelings were often at the "ten" level of intensity. That was not surprising for her. She has been dealing with being abused by her father for years and has faced those feelings in a courageous manner. Following the direction of Awareness Integration provided her with another opportunity to be with those feelings, to release some of the intensity, and to look for new meanings drawn from her experience to apply to her life.

Not surprisingly, her feelings shifted when we began tracking them in this phase. She easily identified fear: "When I come home, I'm afraid he will punish me, and I can't say anything to anybody about it." Then there was deep, deep pain: "Sometime he hugs me and tells me he loves me, and then the abuse . . . it just hurts, hurts, hurts." And then came the sadness, as she allowed her feelings to extend to messages she had taken from those traumatic experiences with her father: "Nobody's love is pure. All the people who come to you and tell you that they love you, they are just fake. There is no love. It's a cruel world."

After Fara spent time realizing the beliefs that she had created based on her experience and started releasing her emotions, those emotions were just as intense as when she was four. As she continued to follow the Awareness Integration trail, a great deal of progress unfolded, which you will see when her name comes up again during our exploration of other life areas.

Is there an important step you might be ready to take from tracking your emotions related to your father now? Identify the key negative core belief and the strongest emotion attached to it that you uncovered here and follow the trail to the exercise in appendix A.

YOUR MOTHER

It's no secret that our relationship with our mother forms a huge part of our identity. After all, we begin life in her womb, so there is an attachment there that begins even before our attachment with our father. From infancy, we are highly sensitive to her manner and ways as a person, especially in her approach to us. Almost any therapeutic work will inevitably focus on our relationship with our mother at some point. So this life area will be especially fruitful in your exploration of Awareness Integration.

For decades, healing professionals have been examining new aspects of the impact of the mother-child relationship. Allan N. Schore, a psychotherapist and internationally recognized researcher, recently brought in theories from neuroscience in his book *Affect Regulation and the Repair of the Self* to shed new light on why those early experiences with our mother leave such an indelible mark on us. As he explains, our experiences from early infancy are received and stored in our right brain, the more intuitive, emotional side.[1] In fact, our mother's emotional response to life situations is sent from her right brain, so it is really a right-brain-to-right-brain transmission.

To me, these findings provide further evidence that so much of the identity and the personality that we create are established in those first months and years with Mom. What her face communicates, and the emotion attached to that state, is something that we take in directly, and we build conclusions on this information. The way we perceive ourselves and the world is formulated in large part by those right-brain receptions.

As an example, if your mother is always smiling and loving while nurturing you, you conclude that the world is a safe and loving place. But if you see her face as constantly anxious, you take in anxiety as a core emotion and a natural response to people and the world. Or if your mother tells you that she loves you but experiences physical pain while breastfeeding you, something you see in her face, you are likely to interpret her experience as evidence that you cause pain: You are unlovable. If your mother often gets angry, you learn anger from her expression. It's the same for sadness, grief, or positive emotions such as love. As an impressionable infant, everything is experienced as either pain or pleasure, comfortable or uncomfortable. Picking up cues from our mother's experience plays a major part in making those distinctions. Then we slowly begin to add meaning to those very early responses. Those meanings stick with us and surface in every aspect of our life.

So as you walk through this life area, perhaps you will have an experience of revisiting a memory in which you can identify one of those influential right-brain transmissions. Or perhaps your discoveries will take you in a different direction. Your enhanced awareness of any part of your relationship with your mother will certainly provide you with further opportunities for healing and growth.

Let's brainstorm just a few preliminary questions and issues before taking on the core questions of Awareness Integration. Similar to your exploration of your relationship with your father, it will be helpful to look at the role you played with your mother and how that role evolved. As a girl, perhaps you went through a rivalry stage with your mom. If so, did that transform into more of a best friend kind of relationship? Or did you get stuck in the conflict? As a boy, did you once look upon Mom as a mate? If so, did you reach the point where you were able to fully let go of her within this role so you could make room for a real-life partner? Did she help you let go, or did she try to hang on?

Did your mother respect you while you were growing up? If so, how did that positive regard assist you in finding your way in the world? If she did not respect you, did you rebel against that stand? Even if you tried to rebel, you may have been caught in the dynamic of how we tend to mimic our parents. So you may want to ask yourself if, in some ways, you followed her mode of behavior that you did not like while not liking it in yourself.

The door to awareness and change related to our relationship with our mother can often be opened when we begin to see our mother from a more well-rounded perspective. In other words, can you see your mom for who she was, a human being dealing with her own influences from her own mother and all her other life experiences? When you recognize that the way she acted toward you was really not about you at all, you can begin to let go of the hardwired identities and conclusions you had taken in through your right brain. I'll offer an example of how this can work when you reach the point of tracking emotions in this section.

For now, let's look at the basic questions of our model.

1. What do you think of your mother?

    So right away you may invite yourself to think about her with fresh eyes. As one human being, what do you think of your mother? Now you can go on to give voice to what you think or have thought of her through the years that may be complimentary but could very well be very harsh and painful.

2. How do you feel about your mother?

    Write both positive/pleasurable and negative/unfavorable emotions. Whether it comes from back then or more recent times, let your true feelings have their full expression here.

3. How do you behave toward your mother?

    As you reflect on how you act toward her, notice any self-questioning of whether you should be acting differently. Is there some guilt or regret seeping through?

4. How does the way you think, feel, and behave toward your mother impact your life and others' lives?

    Has it affected your own sense of mothering, being with authority, or the way you take care of yourself? Do you generalize your views to all women or all mothers?

5. What do you assume your mother thinks about you?

    Does she believe you're a great daughter or son? Does she still look at you as if you were a child? Does she see you as capable or incapable?

6. What do you assume she feels about you?

    I bet you can still see it through your mother's facial expression or her eyes. What words would express those feelings she has about you?

7. How do you experience her behavior toward you?

    Explore it all, what you like and don't like in the way she behaves toward you. Feel free to mention how you wish she would behave toward you, and why.

8. How has the way that you assume your mother thinks, feels, and behaves toward you impacted your life and others' lives?

    Did you follow some path that was forged by her way of relating to you, and what she believed was best for you? Or have you rebelled and tried to be totally different? If so, how has that process worked for you?

9. In your mother's presence, what do you think about yourself?

    Maybe the thought "I'm trying to be the best daughter I know how to be" comes to mind, or "I'm pitiful that I still care so much what she thinks." Follow your own thoughts and beliefs attached to them.

10. In your mother's presence, how do you feel about yourself?

    Perhaps you would say, "I feel small," "I feel helpless," or "I feel grateful that I've finally grown up and can relate to her as an adult." Give expression to your feelings, whatever they happen to be.

11. In your mother's presence, how do you behave toward yourself?

    Do you suddenly begin acting more anxious, or do you lash out in anger at the slightest provocation and then criticize yourself for acting that way?

12. How does the way that you think, feel, and behave toward yourself around your mother impact your life and others' lives?

Maybe you dread your next visit with her. Perhaps you are tired and frustrated by all the times that you have tried to change the dynamics between you. Does it remain even when she is not around? If your mother has passed away, is the impact still prominent, or has it lessened?

AURORA'S STORY

Aurora's mother was bipolar. From the age in which she was able to have some concept of what that meant, she understood this reality as a fact. However, that didn't mean she really grasped the influence of her mother's illness on her mother's life and her relationship with her mom. This level of understanding changed when Aurora followed the Awareness Integration journey. While answering the questions you have just completed, she found herself repeating the phrase "I'm unlovable." So that's what we tracked.

The phrase took Aurora to a vivid memory of when she was four or five years old. One day her mother forgot to pick her up from preschool or kindergarten. Somehow she wound up walking home, alone, in the pouring rain. When she got home, she was struck by her mother's nonchalant response to realizing that she had left her daughter at school. The message Aurora took away was this: "She forgot me and doesn't seem to care. That means she doesn't love me, so I must be unlovable." Her feelings were accentuated by constantly observing how her mother did seem capable of showing love toward her older sister, most likely because that sister had assumed the role of mothering their mom.

After taking time to be with her deep sadness, and beginning to release that emotion, Aurora freed up room to see the memory and the lasting influence in a new light. Her mother was sick, and it was her illness that led her to act the way she did. It was not about Aurora at all. Even her mother's closer relationship to Aurora's sister was steered by her illness. She just needed someone to take care of her. Now the chains were unbound, and Aurora soon became far less judgmental toward herself and others. For the first time in her life she was able to communicate her real feelings, which opened the door to improved relationships with her sister and her friends. She also learned new job and career skills, which she had long resisted because, if you're unlovable, why bother? Her life was moving in powerful new directions.

See where your memories will take you. Find a phrase that represents the negative core belief and the feeling that emerges from it and invite yourself to track that expression now. If you had more than one strong feeling, choose the one that feels the most important to you now, knowing that you can continue the exercise by tracking a second emotion later as you weave your way to your most prominent negative core belief.

Because of the nature of the mother-child relationship, the memories you will bring up will most likely be the first time you ever felt these emotions. Do not be concerned about whether it seems "accurate," since you may not consciously remember much from those early years. The memory, and the feelings and beliefs attached to it, is real. It is there for you to embrace and learn from. Soak it in. Pay particular attention to the conclusions you drew from these early and pivotal experiences. Ask yourself whether that conclusion has any basis in reality for you today. Have you been carrying some self-concept forged in infancy that you can now let go of? Go to appendix A for the full exercise.

YOUR PARENTS' RELATIONSHIP

It's our first representation of mate-hood. Whether our parents had a healthy and enduring marriage, or whether they fought all the time and either divorced or just kept on fighting, they presented an example of relationships that we couldn't help being influenced by. Whatever we saw and experienced in that partnership, and the meaning we took from it, most likely became a blueprint for us in our own relationships. It takes a great deal of awareness, and commitment, to choose something different from that example. Any emotion we had attached to that concept or relationship makes it even more powerful.

So it's essential that we really look at that influence and how it is steering our relationships today. The belief about relationships that we seized as a consequence of what our parents modeled for us is as big as the air we breathe.

Sometimes we have more than our own memories to draw from in considering the state of our parents' relationship. If you have had an opportunity as an adult to ask your parents about their relationship, you might have gained a lot of useful information to apply to your own evaluation of your relationship behavior. What they shared with you may have confirmed what you already knew about how they loved or how and why they clashed. They also may surprise you. Often our parents go to great lengths to conceal truths about their relationship from their children. What we saw on the outside in daily life around them may have been very different from what was happening on the inside. It's also possible that, over the years, their relationship changed in significant ways from how it had been when you were young. If you are very fortunate, your parents may even have learned something about relationships in reviewing their mistakes that could be helpful to you now.

If your parents divorced, you will likely hear different stories from both parties. They may also be willing individually to reflect on their feelings about how their relationship struggles impacted you. Perhaps you will also have the chance to tell them how it was for you. Real opportunities for healing can emerge from these kinds of talks, no matter how long it's been since your childhood years.

Divorce naturally has a profound impact on us as children. We may have blamed ourselves for all that fighting and turmoil, or for the ultimate breakup. We may have also found ourselves siding with one parent or the other. Or we felt alone, scared, or sad. Those feelings will likely have their place during your exploration of this area of the Awareness Integration journey. As well as the personal wounds we may have suffered from divorce or any marital conflict between our parents and the manner in which they dealt with it, we were also left with those negative messages. For children of divorced parents, one of the most frequent conclusions is that marriage is simply not permanent. A loving connection between adults is just not meant to be constant and lasting. Did you adopt any concept like that? And if one or both parents remarried, you've got an entire new adult relationship to review for influences on you.

Observing our parents' marriage may have also imprinted indelible ideas about gender roles. Despite all the cultural movements and changes regarding gender stereotypes and gender-driven roles in marriage that we have witnessed in the last few decades, what we saw with Mom and Dad at home may still be something we hold as the way it is supposed to be. Have you in any way limited your way of being as a man or a woman in relationship because of what you saw in your parents' marriage? Is the man always supposed to be in charge? Is the woman supposed to play the leading role in parenting?

So now it's time to turn your spotlight on the basic questions regarding your parents' relationship. I hope you find some nuggets!

1. What do you think of your parents' relationship?

   You may find yourself answering one way when you consider what you thought about their relationship while you were growing up and another way when you think about it today. Both perspectives are valid and useful.
2. How do you feel about your parents' relationship?

   If you blurt out something such as, "I am always stressed and frustrated; I wish they had gotten divorced!" you know you have some juice to work with here. Or you may report something such as, "I have felt such safety and security; it's amazing they have been able to make it work for forty years."

3. How do you behave toward your parents' relationship?

You may again want to address this question both to your behavior when you were young and to your actions today. You may have needed to shield yourself from the turmoil, as much as possible, while growing up. Is it still that way now? Or do you find yourself playing some role in the middle of their relationship conflict? How is that working for you?

4. How does the way you think, feel, and behave toward your parent's relationship impact your life and others' lives?

The impact may directly connect to your own relationships, or it may show itself in more personal and singular domains. You will know what's true for you.

5. When you are present with your parents, what do you think about yourself?

Perhaps you think, "I am damaged," "I survived war," "I turned out pretty awesome," or "I am the product of love."

6. When you are present with your parents, how do you feel about yourself?

You might say, "I feel sad about living through all that turmoil" or "I am grateful to have been nurtured in their love."

7. When you are present with your parents, how do you behave toward yourself?

Do you ridicule yourself—"I blame myself for their fights"—or praise yourself—"I am the one who brought them together and created peace at home"?

8. How does the way that you think, feel, and behave when you are present with your parents' relationship impact your life and others' lives?

Write the positive and negative impact. Your parent's relation might represent the essence of family. Watch what you do in holidays when you are with family.

So allow yourself to take a closer look at any intense feelings associated with your reflections on your parents' relationship now as you seek to identify your strongest negative core belief. Go to appendix A.

A PRIMARY CARETAKER (NOT A PARENT)

For many of us, our parents were not the only adults that played an important role in shaping our values and character while we were growing up. These next two areas of life on the Awareness Integration journey will provide you with an opportunity to take inventory of one or more of those influential people.

Let's begin with someone who may have assumed the role of a primary caretaker for you during some period of your childhood or adolescence. This could have been a person who stepped in to take on day-to-day care of you if one or both of your parents died or were unable to maintain active parenting. Perhaps it was a grandparent, an aunt or uncle, or a foster parent. That person likely had a profound effect on you. However, even if your parents were both alive and living with you, someone else may have emerged who filled some kind of a void left by your mother and father. In my own life, my mother's cousin became my confidant and was the only adult around me who seemed truly capable of and willing to offer me unconditional love. If she was not there for me during the turbulent years of my parents' fighting and divorce, I feel very certain I would have suffered much more and been far less able to move forward onto the path my life has followed. Just knowing that she was there created a sense of stability for me, which was so critical at that time. Some children have a nanny that fills in what their parents don't bring them.

If you had some kind of additional or substitute caretaker, most likely you have warm memories of that relationship. That figure could have been your one true source of love, guidance, and even motivation or inspiration. If someone in your life fits that description, focus on your thoughts, feelings, and behavior related to your relationship with him or her now. Even though that person does not share your genes, you most likely have seen how your personality was shaped by their influence.

Of course, it's also possible that this substitute caretaker did not have a positive influence on your life. Perhaps you had a stepmother who treated you badly or even traumatized you. This is your chance to safely explore that relationship. I had a client whose mother left the family, prompting her father to bring her to live with her aunt and cousins. That turned out to be a very unhealthy situation that left its imprint on my client. She was able to gain valuable awareness of that situation at this stop of the Awareness Integration journey.

Whoever this caretaker person is in your life, if you had one, spend a few minutes now reflecting on the circumstances present when they got "on stage" with you. Did they arrive because you were looking for someone, or were they assigned to take care of you? Did their appearance take you by surprise? What was it about him or her that most impacted you?

You may also want to consider whether or not this relationship had a lasting place in your life. Did that person stay an important presence for you, or was the relationship only temporary? And if it didn't last, was that okay with you, or did you grieve the loss? If that person supplied love that you didn't get from your parents, did you feel guilty for loving this person more than you loved your mother or father? Or, if the caretaker was assigned to you by your parents and the new relationship proved abusive, did you blame your parents for letting this person in your life?

A key question to ask before we settle into the terrain of the model is this: If this person had not been there, how would your life have turned out differently?

1. What do you think of this primary caretaker?

    Your response may come out as a bold proclamation: "I think I should have had her as my mother!" Find the words that best capture your belief or attitude about this person.

2. How do you feel about this primary caretaker?

    Write both positive/pleasurable and negative/uncomfortable emotions. Perhaps you feel fortunate they were there or maybe you are angry that you had to live with them. How did you feel when you were actively spending time with them?

3. How do you behave toward this primary caretaker?

    If it's no longer an active relationship for you, you can steer the question toward how you behaved toward them when you were with them. You can also approach the question by looking at how you would imagine you would behave toward them if they were still present in your life.

4. How does the way you think, feel, and behave toward this primary caretaker impact your life and others' lives?

    This is where you may name the sweeping characterization of that relationship, for example, "I know he saved my life," or "I would not have even known what love was if it wasn't for her."

5. What do you assume he or she thinks about you?

    Again, you can shift this question to the past, or you can imagine he or she around you today. Of course, your primary caretaker while growing up may still be a part of your life. In that case, you have more direct evidence to call upon.

6. How do you assume he or she feels about you?

    As with our own parents, this is a figure whose feelings were most likely very apparent to you. Did this person feel love toward you, aggravation about you, or compassion for your life situation?

7. How do you experience her or his behavior toward you?

    Maybe this person really listened to you. Perhaps he or she stood up for you when no one else would.

8. How has the way that you assume this primary caretaker thinks, feels, and behaves toward you impacted your life and others' lives?

    Maybe you felt the love and acceptance long after the person was actively engaged in your life. See if you reconnect with that sense now.

9. When you are present with this primary caretaker, what do you think about yourself?

   Perhaps it was as simple as believing that you deserved love. If so, what a wonderful contribution this was to your welfare!

10. When you are present with this primary caretaker, how do you feel about yourself?

    If the person was someone you were not able to see regularly, maybe you felt great sadness when you parted or a deep longing for them to be around more regularly.

11. When you are present with this primary caretaker, how do you behave toward yourself?

    For many people, the presence of this person inspired them to be more nurturing of themselves. What was it for you?

12. How does the way that you think, feel, and behave toward yourself around your primary, nonparent caretaker impact your life and others' lives?

Even if this person has not been actively engaged in your life for thirty years or longer, I bet you have uncovered some feeling and an associated belief to explore. Take a moment to sift through your responses to see what that might be. This might be a pleasant or even joyful memory for you, or it may be something more painful. If you need to release some intense emotions due to a negative belief, then do the tracking exercise in appendix A.

Chapter Seven

Me and Me

So far you have explored your relationship to others. Now it is time to put the lens on your relation to you: the way that you relate to love, addiction, illness, body image, and all that is left of your core beliefs, your strengths, and vulnerabilities. This main identity is running it all. Let's look.

LOVE

We tend to use the word "love" often in our lives, in many different contexts. We make note of the love that we receive and the love that we give. We obsess over whether we are getting enough love and if that certain person really does love us or loves us enough. We worry about whether our children really know that they are loved by us. We say, "I love you" regularly to those closest to us, or we wonder why we're not saying it at all.

In this life area of the Awareness Integration journey, you are going to have an opportunity to spend some time with the concept of love and your associations with it. Responding to the questions in this section may stir feelings of compassion and caring, and it may also trigger feelings of sadness, anger, guilt, or even shame. There is a saying that often comes up in personal-growth circles that says, "Love calls up everything that gets in the way of it." So don't be surprised at whatever direction your thoughts, feelings, and reflections of your behavior may go in here. Your goal is simply to be aware and to look for those negative core beliefs that are getting in the way of love in your life.

You may want to begin by thinking about how you define love. Is it an emotion? Is it a general state of being? Is it an intention of how to be? Is it an action or a series of actions? Is it something that comes and goes in the moment, or a more consistent or permanent state? You're simply exploring your own concepts and ideas.

Next, you may choose to consider how you love. Do you wear your feelings of love on your sleeve? Do you look for multiple ways to express your love? Or is it something quiet, more private, that tends to emerge mostly within intimate situations with those you care about? Do you often feel you can love anybody, even the whole world, or only certain people?

Where is your limit for love? Where do you ever say in your thoughts or actions, "That's it, no more love for me"? Does that limit crop up with both your giving of love and your ability to receive love? Then become aware of what happens after you place those limits on love.

What else do you sometimes or often associate with love? Is it combined with need, pleasure, or pain? Do you sometimes say, "I have to do this in the name of love"? Do you ever use it to justify control? For example, you may say to yourself, "I love my kids so I have to know where they are at all times." Does love seem to always come wrapped with a sense of duty, obligation, or responsibility? Or do you believe that you show it and share it freely?

Take a moment also to reflect on what self-love means to you. Can you name several ways of expressing self-love, and do you practice them enough? Do you hold self-love at the same level of importance as your ability to love others? If not, what beliefs hold you back from building a stronger foundation of self-love? Perhaps you have taken on a belief that self-love is selfish. If so, it may be helpful to remind yourself that investing in loving yourself does not mean that you do not love others. On the flip side, though, if you choose self-love within a conflict with someone you know well, perhaps you are using it as a statement that you are only going to care for yourself, no matter what that feels like for the other person.

Have you sometimes believed that you can't trust love, especially in intimate relationships? If we feel burned by love, we often react by holding ourselves back the next time we sense that love is in the air. This is something that may have come up for you in intimate and romantic relationships, but you may find it emerging again here, in a different light. Without thinking of any particular person, it can be revealing to simply ask yourself, "What does it mean to me to trust love?"

So let's plunge into the pool of love and see how the waters feel for you.

1. What do you think of love?

    Without necessarily relating it to yourself, what do you think of love as a general idea? Is it a good thing, or is it a dangerous thing? Is it real, or is it just a mirage, something conjured up to sell Hallmark greeting cards?

Your core beliefs may begin to pop up here: "I feel incapable of really loving"; "I feel I have allowed myself to be fooled in the name of love"; or "I'm excited about my new love interest in my life."

2. How do you feel about love?

Perhaps you would say, "I love loving," "I feel sad when I love," or "I always have lots of anxiety and fear when I feel love or others love me."

3. How do you behave toward love?

Do you find yourself tip-toeing around love, or do you let it pour out of every fiber of your being? Does love make you act differently from how you usually behave, perhaps by resorting to a younger, more carefree, more playful attitude?

4. How does the way you think, feel, and behave toward love impact your life and others' lives?

Has love brought you forward in life, or has it held you back as you have yielded to fear about expressing it? Maybe love, especially self-love, has been a great protector for you. If so, how? Have you mixed in too many other things with love?

5. What do you assume other people think of you in relation to love?

Do they see you as the most loving person they know? Do they believe you are too quick to open your heart and freely love someone when the evidence suggests that you will get hurt? Do they think you need to do a better job of loving yourself?

6. How do you assume other people feel about you in relation to love?

Do they feel envious of your ability to love? Do they feel jealous that you seem to attract love much more easily than they can? Do people close to you love you all the more because of how they feel loved by you?

7. How do other people behave toward you in relation to love?

Do people come toward you because of your style of loving and your willingness to share it, or do they keep their distance because they sense that your love may overwhelm or smother them? Do people sometimes back away from you because they see you as someone not able to recip-rocate love?

8. How does the way that you assume other people think, feel, and behave toward you in relation to love impact your life and others' lives?

This is an area where it's extremely difficult to ignore how others relate to us. We often think of love as the emotion at the core of our be-ing so if others judge us or protect themselves from us because of how they see us as a loving person, it can really get under our skin. So take an extra moment to consider how you have been impacted by family, lovers, close friends, or anyone else where love has been a part of your connection.

9. When you are present with love, what do you think about yourself?

   This is where your judgments about how much or how well you love is likely to surface. Whether those judgments are positive or negative, do your best to allow them their expression. Do you give yourself credit for being more able to love today than when you were younger?

10. When you are present with love, how do you feel about yourself?

   Maybe you notice that your feelings relate to changes in how you have loved over time. Do you feel grand and gracious, or do you feel stuck? Does love bring out sadness for you, or does it usher in a sense of oneness?

11. When you are present with love, how do you behave toward yourself?

   Does the experience of feeling really loved by someone else make you want to jump up and dance? Or does it make you want to recoil, guarding against what could come next? Do you blame yourself for loving too much or too little?

12. How does the way that you think, feel, and behave toward yourself when you are around love impact your life and others' lives?

   It no doubt extends beyond your most loving relationships. When we feel confident in our ability to give and receive love, it sends ripples throughout our life. And if we have any kind of negative connotation with love, it similarly will add more bricks to the wall of protectiveness or pain.

Look for your own "aha!" that may be right there awaiting your awareness now as you choose a feeling, or a strong negative statement, associated with an emotion, to take you back to an earlier memory. If you uncover a painful trauma, remember the option to visit a professional therapist to help you work with it. Go to appendix A to track your negative core belief and emotions if necessary.

ILLNESSES, DISABILITIES, AND ADDICTIONS

All along the Awareness Integration trail, you have been exploring your relationships with many different people in your life. You have also looked at your relationship to things you do such as your work or the way you are with money and sex. Now we're going to zero in on something you may have as part of your daily life. Specifically, I am inviting you to consider any ongoing illness, disability, or addiction you may be challenged with.

Now, before you quickly declare, "none of this applies to me" because you don't have any physical or mental disability or condition and you are not an alcoholic or drug addict, slow down for a moment. With addictions, we're going to broaden the inquiry beyond addictions to alcohol or substances. Let's tune into this simple reality: Most of us are addicted to something. It may be cigarettes, sugar, or caffeine. It may be an addiction or obsession related to your behavior: shopping, TV watching, texting or Internet surfing, and so forth. These are practices that can cause harm to yourself or others and yet you continue to do it, with no firm control on stopping. So take careful consideration of what you do in an obsessive way that may be holding you back from living fully or actualizing important goals.

If you currently have an active addiction to alcohol or drugs, in order to fully benefit from the Awareness Integration journey you need to be sober for at least three months, working on your recovery, and gaining support from a counselor or therapist. If you have not taken those steps, get help today!

Whatever your addiction or obsession happens to be, you can learn a great deal about your life by asking our basic questions about it: What do you think about that addiction or obsession? How do you feel about it? How do you behave toward it? And then you can look at that addiction as a part of you: What does that addictive part of you think and feel about you? So stay with us here. More than likely, this life area really does apply to you.

If you do happen to be dealing with an illness or some other physical disability or challenge, or some kind of mental health condition, here's your chance to gain awareness about that by looking at it in what may be a new way. The first question to consider is this: What type of identity do you attach to this illness or condition? If you were born with a physical disability, for example, you might have carried a degree of shame for having it. But then that shame may have turned into a sense of entitlement: "I need to be taken care of in a special way." Or you may have found yourself voicing resentment: "It's not fair that I have to deal with this!" As you have gone on in life, have you found yourself fighting the condition or gradually accepting it? Or did your relationship with this condition evolve into something positive?

If you have grappled with a mental disability or condition, perhaps you have carried more of a stigma for having it. In contrast to a physical disability, which usually can be recognized by others just by looking at you, a mental disability or condition may not be immediately visible. That might lead you to feel more anxious about having the condition and then dealing with the reaction of others when they become aware of it.

If your disability or condition is something that came along much more recently, as opposed to a condition you had from birth or childhood, what challenges did you face in coming to grips with your changed state? How did your identity get reshaped by what happened, and how did people begin to relate to you differently because of, say, HIV, ADHD, or a bipolar diagnosis? Often people respond to those with a condition such as Alzheimer's with compassion, while their approach with someone wrestling with cancer or heart disease might be to offer advice about treatment approaches to pursue.

With an addiction or obsession, it's quite possible that others in your life have been better able to recognize and name the issue than you have. What do you say when you hear them point out your addiction or obsessive behavior? Do you deny, defend, and counterattack? If you have rebuffed their suggestions, perhaps you can approach this life area as an experiment. You can view this possible addiction from the lens of, "If this really is an addiction or obsession for me, how do I feel about it?" And keep going with the questions.

Often a mental or physical disability or condition becomes almost a branding: Your life is reoriented with this condition at the center of it. It seemingly defines you, coloring almost everything you do and believe. Over time, though, this reorientation may open the door to an opportunity for growth. Successfully handling this condition and its limitations on your life may instill self-confidence, with your achievements on this front trumping almost all others in your life in importance because of what you had to do to achieve it. After working our way through grief, anger, denial, and all those other phases, we may reach a state of acceptance that delivers us to a whole new perspective on how life can be. We may look at others and the world with greater compassion and understanding, and we may find new ways to utilize our unique gifts.

So no matter what phase you find yourself in as you deal with some physical or mental condition or addiction, take a few moments to assess your own relationship with this challenging situation. We'll begin with the questions geared toward physical and mental conditions, and then rephrase the questions for those with addictions.

1. What do you think of your illness, disability, or condition?

   "I think God doesn't love me or he wouldn't have given this to me"; "I know I have cancer because of all the chemicals they put in our food." These are just a couple of the many beliefs I have heard at this stage. Does yours sound anything like that, or do you carry more of an accepting attitude?

2. How do you feel about your illness, disability, or condition?

   Are you angry at the illness? Are you angry at God? Be honest. These are just your feelings. Do you get frustrated about what you can't do or how slowly things seem to change despite your best treatment? Do you worry about your family and how they are being impacted by your condition?

3. How do you behave toward your illness, disability, or condition?

   Do you rebel against it, or do you try to befriend it as part of your life? Do you regard it as a challenge that you must battle against with every ounce of your being?

4. How does the way you think, feel, and behave toward your illness, disability, or condition impact your life and others' lives?

    Your answer may go in many different directions for you, especially if this has been a longtime challenge. Giving voice to what you imagine the future impact will be may also be relevant for you here.

5. When people you know are around you in dealing with this condition, what do you assume they think about you?

    Do they think you're brave? Do they think they should do something to help you? Or do they think you are in denial?

6. When people you know are around you in dealing with this condition, how do you assume they feel about you?

    Is it sadness or even pity? Or something closer to respect or admiration? Do they feel scared about having something like that come into their own lives? Or do they feel angry that their relationship with you has been affected by this condition?

7. When people you know are looking at you in dealing with this condition, how do you experience their behavior toward you?

    Have they stuck with you or backed away? Do they display great patience or occasional annoyance?

8. How has your life and the lives of others been impacted by the way that you assume people think, feel, and behave toward you when they are around you in dealing with your condition?

    Again, this may bring up sadness or disappointment about the response of others. But maybe you have cultivated new relationships through support groups for those battling the same illness or condition.

9. What do you think about yourself in regard to your illness, disability, or condition?

    Do you sometimes think it's all your fault, that you "created" this condition? Or do you hold to a belief that there will come a better day?

10. How do you feel about yourself in regard to your illness, disability, or condition?

    Do you like yourself because you are doing the best you can, or do you judge yourself for not having a better attitude or for not following the plan of how to deal with this life challenge? If you sometimes feel helpless or hopeless, how do you respond to the presence of these natural emotions?

11. How do you behave toward yourself in regard to your illness, disability, or condition?

    Do you frequently decide that you need to escape and dull your senses with TV or computer games? Or do you make an attempt to find constructive ways to confront the tougher days, perhaps by bringing humor to your situation?

12. How does the way that you think, feel, and behave when you are present with your illness, disability, or condition impact your life and others' lives?

    Maybe it has instilled in you a desire to help other people. Or perhaps it has contributed to shying away from the kinds of goals you still may be able to achieve. Is there a way to get past those limitations triggered by discouragement?

Track your emotions and negative thoughts through the exercise in appendix A. Sometimes we begin with one feeling, such as anger, but when we hold up that anger for greater scrutiny it quickly shifts to something different, perhaps embarrassment. It's fine to track the new emotion because that may reveal something beneath the surface, but you may still want to check in with that anger afterward. So if you're hearing a chorus of "It's not fair! It's not fair!" then it will pay to listen to the anger—or sadness—that's playing the music.

What happens here may surprise you. Although you may attach your belief about unfairness to the cancer that invaded your life five years ago, your memory of unfairness may usher you straight back to childhood when you were penalized for something you believe you didn't do. If you can breathe into that feeling, and assign a different meaning to what happened back then, you may be better equipped to regard your cancer in a more grounded way today.

For those who are addressing some kind of addiction or obsessive behavior, here's the form in which those questions will be the most effective for you. Notice that the first and third sets of questions are essentially the same as in dealing with a physical or mental condition. The second part proceeds in a different manner:

1. What do you think of your addiction?

    Would you say it's "the worse enemy of my life" or "my best buddy through thick and thin"?

2. How do you feel about your addiction?

    Would you say "shame, disgust, powerless, and guilt" or "pleasure, joy, and connectedness"?

3. How do you behave toward your addiction?

    Perhaps you would say, "I slave under it and can't resist it; I fight with it and I lose" or "I feed it and let it run the show."

4. How does the way you think, feel, and behave toward your addiction impact your life?

    For the next series of questions, try that approach that I mentioned about looking at that addiction or obsession as a part of you.

5. When this addictive part is looking at you, what do you assume it thinks about you?

It might think that you are slow to see its real needs: connection, life engagement, and spiritual fulfillment. Often those are the kinds of authentic life needs that became distorted through some addictive or obsessive behavior.

6. When this addictive part is looking at you, how do you assume it feels about you?

Maybe it's a feeling response driven by a judgment: "I'm disappointed that she has no willpower." Or maybe your addictive part is more re-signed: "It's sad that he just keeps escaping from his real-life issues, but I guess I just have to keep feeding him his escape because he's not ready to change."

7. When this addictive part is looking at you, how does it behave toward you?

Is it playful and beckoning? Does it bargain with you for "just a little more" or pull you along because "it's not so bad to do this sometimes?"

8. How has your life and others' lives been impacted by what you assume this addictive part thinks, feels, and behaves toward you?

Perhaps the key consideration is whether that addictive part is ruling your life, and if so, are you willing to take more personal responsibility? If your addictive part is in conflict with another, healthier part of you, how can you bring those parts into a dialogue to meet both their needs in a way that serves your greater good? This is something that can begin to unfold during the phase of tracking emotions in this life area.

9. When you are present with your addiction, what do you think about yourself?

10. When you are present with your addiction, how do you feel about yourself?

11. When you are present with your addiction, how do you behave toward yourself?

12. How does the way that you think, feel, and behave when you are present with your addiction impact your life?

Again, even if you are acting "as if" an addiction or obsession might be operative in your life, as others claim it is, your honest responses here will certainly contribute to your awareness.

Carefully review all your responses in this entire section. Again, even though this relationship with some mental or emotional condition or life challenge is not with another person, it's likely that this exploration has stirred feelings in you. Perhaps you can easily circle one charged emotional statement or belief or spot a trend that can be boiled down into one revealing attitude, concept, or identity. This is your opportunity to pursue that phrase or feeling a bit further. It may turn out to be a negative core belief that, when you track and release it, takes you on an important step in your awareness and growth. Also, if your exploration of your feelings uncovers some desire or pull that may threaten your recovery, be sure to call upon your trusted support system to help you. Track your core belief and the emotional charge in your body by going to appendix A.

BEING WITH YOURSELF, LOOKING AT THE MIRROR

It's been a long journey down the Awareness Integration path, hasn't it? You have come in contact with many different people that you know, and you've looked at circumstances and situations from several different realms of life. Now you've reached a critical crossroads. You are about to come face-to-face with yourself.

We're going to spend extra time in this life area because, as you might expect, important attitudes and beliefs about yourself are likely to emerge. The emotions that greet you here will be especially significant and valuable to trace because, by this point in the journey, your emotional work in the previous life areas has helped you to clean up and clear out a whole lot of stored emotions and the negative core beliefs associated with them. The beliefs and feelings that will show up here are the really persistent ones—as if the words that are spoken in this life area sound more definitive, a seemingly nonnegotiable concept or belief. Inviting these words and feelings in, and bringing awareness to them, can have a pivotal role in releasing not only old beliefs but also old patterns, the kind of patterns that hold you down and keep you stuck. This is a close-up look only at you, and there's no running away from it.

I invite you to approach this stop in two different ways. The first is to get an actual mirror and look at yourself in that mirror. Then respond to the same questions we have been asking as you literally see yourself face-to-face. After that process is complete, I invite you to close your eyes and imagine that the path you have been traveling on throughout your Awareness Integration journey has changed into a tunnel. And as you walk into that tunnel, you notice mirrors on all sides, the top, and the bottom. If you look up, you see yourself. When you look down, you see yourself. And if you look left or right, you still see yourself.

If you're like most people whom I have guided into this life area, you will likely respond to what you see in a visual way. In other words, body image rises to your awareness. Well, I've never met anyone who says they have a perfect body, so there's a pretty good chance you will encounter some negative belief there. What is it for you? Are you not attractive enough? Do you need to lose weight or gain weight? Is your nose, hips, or butt too big? Are you too pale or too dark skinned? If you're a man, are you losing too much hair? If you're a woman, is your hair not looking right, or are your breasts somehow not the right size?

Many issues relating to body image have come wrapped in heaps of ridicule, potentially going all the way back to school days. Or the issue may have entered your life at a later time: You were thin as a child but obese as an adult. So you've got the reactions of other adults to absorb. If something did change in your physical appearance, you may be carrying anger or resentment about that. As you sort out the messages you have received about how you look, inquire as to who created them. Was it your friends, your community, the culture, or yourself? Did the message come via a trauma?

Simply note all these observations regarding your beliefs about physical appearance, and then get ready for an extra challenge: Remove your clothing and look at yourself in the mirror while naked. Now you really can't hide from yourself!

Look more closely at your own eyes looking back at you. From that place, ask yourself the questions about how you think and feel, and watch what comes quickly to mind. "I'm bad." "I hate myself." "I'm useless and will never amount to anything." Those are the deeply ingrained beliefs and feelings that are most crying out for your attention now.

Of course, your answers may sound more neutral: "I am who I am, for better or worse." Or perhaps they will even come out in a positive light: "I'm kindhearted and loving." In fact, you just might discover that your self-concept has already shifted in a more positive direction from doing the work of the previous life areas of Awareness Integration. Good for you!

Whatever you experience is real for you. When you do see a negative attitude pop up on your radar, ask yourself, "How well is this attitude working for me in my life?" If you could choose another attitude or approach, what would it be? If you have run into charged emotions, I urge you to take your time going through each of them individually when you reach that part of this life area. If you do so, I strongly suspect that you will reap major dividends.

Complete all the questions while looking at yourself in the mirror. If you did remove your clothing, you are of course welcome to get dressed again! Then close your eyes. Once more, imagine that the path you have been following on your Awareness Integration journey has changed into a tunnel and all around you in every direction in this tunnel are mirrors. Track the same questions again. Note this time how your answers may be defining or capturing your self-esteem. This is the essence of what you think about yourself. That's why the awareness that you will gain in your experience that is about to begin here can be so powerful.

FARA'S STORY (PART 3)

You may recall my client Fara and her exploration of her trauma triggered by the abuse she suffered with her father. When she reached this life area, Fara struggled to even look at the mirror I brought out. Her self-esteem issues were very strong, and she had been "looking at herself" in many ways and contexts throughout her experience with the Awareness Integration journey. But she was committed to her work, and she stayed with the varied emotions that tugged at her: sadness, shame, and pity. Then she connected with a deep, deep tiredness. She was just tired of her life, she told me. She had no thoughts of committing suicide; she was simply weary of feeling those negative feelings about herself and tired of believing that she couldn't get herself moving forward to create change.

When I invited Fara to track this feeling, no memory emerged. It may work that way for you sometimes as well. But something was slowly softening in her usually stiff negative stance. She didn't break through any walls yet, but her willingness to stick with her experience was planting the seeds for changes to come as the journey continued.

Let's see what shape this valuable material will take for you now.

1. As you look at yourself in the mirror, what do you think?

   If your first response sounds something like, "I'd rather not be doing this at all," wait for the words and messages linked to the desire to avert your gaze.

2. As you look at yourself in the mirror, how do you feel?

   Perhaps the answers will relate your age: "I feel really old" or "I hate all that gray hair." You might try blinking your eyes a few times, looking at the mirror image of yourself again, and inquiring once more how you really feel.

3. As you look at yourself in the mirror, how do you behave toward yourself?

   Are you smiling or laughing? Or are you grimacing and scowling? What's behind that response?

4. How does the way you think, feel, and behave toward yourself as you look at yourself in the mirror impact your life and others' lives?

   Look for connections here. If you have thoughts and feelings about being too fat, has it kept you obsessing about weight-loss methods and holding you back in social situations? If the person you see reflected in the mirror is someone who lacks self-confidence, how might that be blocking your way in achieving your goals and cultivating more joy?

5. When the you in the mirror is looking back at you, what do you assume he or she thinks about you?

    Your responses may be very similar to what you noted in the first round, but they could be different. By turning the reflection in the mirror into a separate entity, the messages that you get back may sound more like the voices of your parents, your peers at school, or the lover who broke up with you. Just notice what bubbles up and try to be present with it.

6. When the you in the mirror is looking at you, how do you assume she or he feels about you?

    Perhaps you would say, "she hates me" or "he thinks I'm a fool." If feelings like that turn up here, you will want to consider working with them in the tracking emotions phase.

7. When the you in the mirror is looking at you, how do you experience his or her behavior toward you?

    Does she act as if she wants to hang out with you or keep her distance? Is he or she encouraging you to change your expression?

8. How has the way that you assume the you in the mirror thinks, feels, and behaves toward you impacted your life and others' lives?

    If the "mirror, mirror on the wall" refrain has captured something deeply painful, stick with it. See how you can bring awareness to it.

All kinds of experiences may be possible for you here. It works this way for many clients: The work you have already done with the Awareness Integration process is revealed in a positive image in the mirror. Of course, the mirror also can serve to bring up significant issues still to be examined.

Now it's your turn to make your own discoveries as you highlight a statement that represents a negative core belief and continue to track your emotions through the exercise in appendix A.

As you move on from visiting with yourself in the mirror in your home and the tunnel of mirrors in your mind, consider whether any deep emotional work that arises is a signal for you to seek out a therapist for support.

Also, if you identified a belief that has remained entrenched for much of your life, perhaps you can now see how it has turned into a formula: "I'll never get anyone to really find me attractive." So therefore you carry an attitude that you're not worth looking at and you don't take proper care of your body. As a result, you become less and less attractive and your self-worth and self-confidence remain low or dip even lower.

Look through your responses to see if you can detect any formula that you have been following. Then name at least ten ways or times that formula has influenced your life, while asking the following key question: How well has this formula been working or not working for me? This is still another approach to name what drives our thoughts, feelings, and behavior in life and hold it up to a higher light. That's where you may notice the glimmer of a possibility to change it.

DANIEL'S JOURNEY (PART 2)

Daniel, the client who was yearning for his first real intimate relationship with a woman when he began his Awareness Integration journey, had a profound experience when he reached the tunnel of mirrors.

"I feel like I've become a pretty confident, fun person," he said. "I'm more outspoken. Before when I would look at myself, I wasn't sure who I was. I'm more comfortable with me now. It's a big difference."

Why did he see a change? Daniel had done some fruitful work in the life area focused on current intimate and romantic relationships in his life. His deeper awareness of what triggered his insecurity and anxiety enabled him to create a shift in his self-concept in this realm. He had been practicing new ways of being with young women, and he liked the initial results. That's what was reflected back to him in the mirror.

Chapter Eight

Beyond the "I"

So far you have focused your attention on relationships with other human beings and yourself. Now it is time to take your attention toward the areas beyond you and human beings: nature, the universe, God, spirit, and death. You are in nature and the universe whether you pay attention to it or not. You are born and raised into one or multiple ideas about God and spirituality, and it forms part of your beliefs. And you face death every day by hearing it on the media, losing a pet, losing a loved one, and finally your own. Let's explore.

BEING IN NATURE AND THE UNIVERSE

"If you are feeling anxious or sad, try going for a quiet walk in the woods." Have you ever heard this advice? Do you sometimes give it to yourself? Do you ever find that you benefit not only physically but also mentally and emotionally, even spiritually, from spending time in nature?

For most of us, there's just something about being in nature that helps us to relax. In nature we are often able to let go, to allow our troubled thoughts to slowly subside and more peaceful thoughts to enter in. When we're walking amidst tall trees, listening to a babbling brook, watching the crashing ocean, or simply gazing out at a vast and beautiful view, life somehow seems bigger than our private struggles, challenges, and frustrations. We become more at ease, and in doing so we have the opportunity to view our own life from a different perspective.

That's one major reason that this life area will be valuable for you as you continue along the Awareness Integration journey. Spending time with nature and asking the questions you have been asking at all the other life areas may simply help you relax and take a breath from the work you have been doing.

More important, feeling more at ease may open the door to a new piece of awareness, something that did not emerge while spending time with people that you know. Here it's just you and nature. The reminder that life is bigger than you can liberate you from more rigid beliefs and patterns.

Where do you most often connect with nature? Do you love being near or in the water, whether it's the ocean, a lake or pond, or just a river or stream? Do you prefer the mountains, whether looking up at the high peaks or driving or hiking to a vista or summit and looking down below? Do you like to immerse yourself in the deep woods or even the simple sanctuary of the green space in your favorite public park? Also, how do you respond to the presence of animals that live in the natural world? What is your general attitude toward nature's creatures?

Take a few moments to consider where you and nature come together and what happens for you when you make that connection. Your reflections may help you uncover important information while responding to the core questions. Remember, as always, that your answers are true for you, regardless of how they seem to fit or not fit with how you believe others think, feel, and behave. So if you find that being in nature stirs loneliness for you rather than promoting a sense of peace and oneness, that is an important awareness for you.

There's another reason that being with nature in your work with Awareness Integration may be impactful. As you continue this journey, you are becoming more aware of the need to be more responsible and accountable in all realms of your life. This accountability extends to your relationship with nature. After all, we are part of nature and in constant relationship with it, although as a culture and as individuals we sometimes forget this is true.

So in this life area you may be considering how committed you are to honoring and preserving nature. Do you recycle? Do you waste water, or do you take great care in shutting it off when not absolutely needed, including limiting time in the shower? Sometimes we get caught up in only thinking about what nature does for us but give little consideration to what we can, or should, do for nature. We really do have a relationship with nature, even if we don't happen to be someone who takes those ten-mile walks in the woods. So you can explore what that relationship with nature is for you personally and what changes, if any, you might like to make.

Now let's take a further step out of yourself and your individual world to connect with something bigger. I am going to invite you to imagine yourself being lifted off the earth and being present out there in the grand universe.

Many fascinating thoughts and feelings may come to you during this experience. You may find yourself remembering back to being a child and sitting on the grass while gazing up at the stars or the moon and dreaming or imagining yourself in a life that was grander, more exciting, or more mysterious than what you knew at the time. Did you ever have childhood moments like that? Where did your dreams take you?

Being in the universe may take you out of the limited roles that you play in your life and connect you back to a sense of your own essence. You ask, "Who am I really in this great big universe?" The answers may surprise you.

In my work with clients at this stop, I have noticed that their beginning approach to imagining being in the universe takes one of three forms: (1) standing in their body and looking up at the universe; (2) being in their body while being somewhere "up there"; and (3) being out of their body and imagining themselves as a very, very small speck or atom. Those who followed the first approach were usually those who related to life in a more concrete way, while those who followed the second approach tended to be more abstract, and those following the third approach were people who often become enmeshed with others and lose their personal boundaries. Rest assured that there's no right or wrong way to shape your experience here. The idea is to just close your eyes for a moment and connect with some image of yourself being with the universe, and then open your eyes and ask the core questions of the model.

If you have ever done a meditation in which you were guided to experience a sense of being at one with the world, or the universe, this process may seem familiar. Whether you found yourself moving from smallness to grandness in your perception of life or you simply came up empty, you no doubt learned something from that meditation or guided imagery. If this experience is quite new for you, I trust you will also learn something meaningful.

As with being with nature, you may find that being in the universe is very liberating. You may easily begin to detach from known associations with your life. While you assess one or more of your most difficult problems you may conclude, "It's not really about me after all" or it's just the "more mundane stuff of life" while something bigger is going on in the large universe. Even the experience of detaching only a little can serve as a reminder that you have that ability in your life: You can let go of at least part of what pulls you down. Being out there in the universe reinforces the notion that you are really just on your own journey, separate and apart from some relationship conflict or issue that clings to you and causes you pain. Any troubling matter can be seen in a different context because who you are in the universe may be different from who you are on your own.

1. What do you think of nature and the universe?

    Try to refrain from making the politically correct statement that pays homage to the value of nature. Respond with your own first thoughts, whatever they may happen to be. As always, your thoughts may have less to do with nature or the universe itself and more to do with you.

2. How do you feel about nature and the universe?

   If you are someone who regularly benefits from time in nature, and you have favorite natural areas, this is your time to give full voice to what you feel about that. Do you feel totally free and unchained? Do you feel happy and light? Or do you feel humbled, lonely, or even sad? Perhaps you feel disoriented and yearn for the safety of having your feet planted firmly on the ground again. Scan your "control panel" for your true feelings while you're up there.

   If your responses begin to take the form of a poem or some other creative expression, feel free to express that.

3. How do you behave toward nature and the universe?

   Do you respect it, or do you ignore it? What specific actions illustrate your manner of behaving toward nature? Of course, your reflections may vary depending on the kind of nature area you have in mind. For me, I love being in water and act with joy and playfulness there, but if you put me in front of a mountain I will just shrug with boredom at this "pile of brown dirt." Some people report wanting to sing and dance and proclaim, "I'm never going back!" Others report a desire to study the sky or the earth below with an exceptionally close eye, so as not to miss the grandeur and the meaning behind it.

4. How does the way you think, feel, and behave toward nature and the universe impact your life and others' lives?

   Does nature restore and reinvigorate you? Does it remind you that there are bigger needs than yours? Do you wish you spent more quality time with nature so that its positive effect would shine through more regularly? Does life back on earth seem as if it has greater possibilities? What one possibility might be waiting for you to act upon right now?

5. In relation to being in nature and the universe, what do you think about yourself?

   You might think, "I am at one with the world around me"; "I make too much of my little problems"; "I'm really a good person"; or "I need to slow down." What are the key phrases that capture your attitude about yourself as stirred by nature or the universe?

6. In relation to being in nature and the universe, how do you feel about yourself?

   If, while imagining yourself spending time with nature or the universe, you are smiling or wrapping your arms lovingly around yourself, what are the emotions being expressed?

7. In relation to being in nature and universe, how do you behave toward yourself?

Perhaps you are more patient or accepting of yourself? Maybe you are inspired to treat yourself with greater care and compassion? Note your own behavior.

8. How does the way that you think, feel, and behave about yourself in relation to nature and the universe impact your life and others' lives?

Again, you may find yourself validating nature for how it leaves you feeling better about yourself. On the other front related to this life area, you may find yourself feeling more inspired to make changes in how you relate to nature or the universe. Is there a nature-oriented organization or a cause you want to join or contribute to?

Because this is often a peaceful respite on the Awareness Integration journey, you may not find any charged emotional statements that you feel inclined to explore. That is fine. Again, simply gaining awareness of your thoughts, feelings, and behavior while in the presence of nature can be enormously valuable. However, if you found yourself feeling angry or frustrated about how "I'm a jerk because I don't do enough to care for nature," "I am so lonely in this big universe," or "I am so small and powerless," that may be something you will want to examine while employing the tools we call upon in this phase of working in any life area (see appendix A).

You also may choose to simply spend time with a more positive or neutral feeling that came up here. A statement such as "I don't need to worry about that old problem anymore because life is bigger than that" may beckon you to simply close your eyes and breathe into that sensation.

BEING WITH GOD

When I guide clients along the Awareness Integration trail, some of the most fascinating moments happen when that person is spending time being with God. I remember working with one man who made it very clear at the outset of this life area that he was an atheist. "I do not believe in God at all," he declared. Still, I urged him to take on the questions related to this stop, and he agreed, somewhat reluctantly. When I asked him how he felt about God, an anger bordering on rage flared up.

"It's not fair!" he shouted. "Look at the world today. There is so much poverty, so much suffering." When I interjected that I thought he was an atheist, he bit his lip and then muttered, "Well, if there is a God, I am angry with him."

This client's experience served as a reminder that almost all of us have had some religious or spiritual belief or concept penetrate our lives. Our culture, like many cultures around the globe, is alive with varied and often passionate ideas and practices related to God. From childhood through adulthood, we come face-to-face with the beliefs of our family, our community, our friends, our political leaders, and people we come across in almost every realm of life. Amid all those influences, we somehow find our way to our own sense of God, even as it may change.

Did you imagine God to be something like a good and all-loving parent, someone you could hold your hands up high to and implore, "Please help me"? Or did you suffer trauma that you associated with God, leaving you holding the seemingly unanswerable question, "If God is good, why does he bring me all this pain and suffering?" Did you commit yourself to pleasing God, or did you feel you were inherently bad and could never be accepted by God? Perhaps that carried into the guilt that often surfaces in the Judeo-Christian tradition, leaving you to conclude, "What I've done is unforgivable,

NAZ'S EXPERIENCE

Naz had a profound emotional experience in this area. When she stood beside God, she revealed that she was afraid of God because he would punish her for being bad. Of course, the punishment was actually delivered by her father and his abusive behavior. Looking further, she found herself saying, "I didn't get any love from God because I always thought I didn't deserve that love."

She identified powerlessness as the feeling behind this statement. Now she was zeroing in on that important negative core belief. In tracking this emotion, she went back to childhood memories of constantly praying to God for help. When she didn't receive the help she requested, she concluded that God didn't love her and that she was undeserving of love. That left her feeling small and powerless. She displayed her willingness to simply be with this feeling, which brought her a degree of calmness about this conflicted relationship. Her release of this sense of powerlessness helped to open the door to a possible new story—one about God, about herself, about who she really was, and about how she could live. Each time she released these feelings as part of her Awareness Integration experience, while looking fully at where they had come from, that new story was coming closer and closer to her reach.

and I am doomed to hell." Did those early beliefs stick you with and become systemized in your life, or did you defy those teachings and follow a path toward claiming your own ideas about God and how you would act upon them?

As you explore your thoughts, feelings, and behavior in this life area, you may find that guilt or shame is part of your God story. Of course, you may also find, or confirm, that you have a positive image of God and that you enjoy the fruits of an affirming relationship with the Almighty. Your belief in God may help to provide a sense of purpose or meaning to your life. Your sense of being in the grace of God may help you to feel not only supported but also empowered. As a co-creator with God, you may feel more able to serve as an agent for good. Tapping the power of your relationship with God may also connect you to the kinds of virtues that all humans strive for as you imagine living closer and closer to an ideal self.

Part of your experience in being with God may also be to examine the expectations you have of God and the expectations you believe God has of you. Are those expectations fair or unfair, and consistent or inconsistent?

Perhaps you will discover that being with God in this way reveals a deeper honesty about how you see yourself and your life. If so, how do you feel about that more honest self-portrait, and what do you choose to do with it?

So whether the idea of spending time being with God is very familiar to you or something you would seldom initiate, I invite you to move into this life area with an open spirit.

1. What do you think of God?

    Remember, the question is asking what you think of God, not what your religion thinks or says about God.
2. How do you feel about God?

    If those feelings have changed over the years, or even day to day, allow yourself to freely float among the different emotions and record them as best as you can. Then, you might ask yourself, "How do I really feel about God right now?"
3. How do you behave toward God?

    Write both actions/behaviors that have created favorable results and the ones that have created unfavorable results. Do you relate to God as a sacred friend, a guide, an inspiration, or a source of comfort? Do you look to God for answers?
4. How does the way you think, feel, and behave toward God impact your life and others' lives?

    I mentioned earlier the experience of an atheist discovering that his perception of God, indeed, had an influence on his life. This has been true for other clients who said they didn't believe in God or held a more doubting,

agnostic view. The impact of God on them still surfaced as they worked
with the model. One woman said, "If God was real, I would fight with
him." So trace the impact for you, regardless of what you believe or do
not believe about God.

5. What do you assume God thinks of you?

 Write your positive and negative assumptions. Those images of how
we are looked upon by God tend to be very powerful. Take your time
focusing on your sense of what God thinks of you.

6. How do you assume God feels about you?

 If your first response is simply, "I know that God loves me," you
might take the next step and consider how God loves you, or when God
loves you most. You will know what direction to follow.

7. How do you experience God's behavior toward you?

 Do you believe that God saves you from tragedy or extreme hardship?
Or do you see God as punishing you, or perhaps acting indifferently toward you because you don't deserve better?

8. How has the way that you assume God thinks, feels, and behaves toward
you impacted your life and others' lives?

 Some people maintain that God is shaping their lives in every way.
Others would conclude that God is too busy to pay them much attention
and thus does not have a dramatic impact on their life. There is a wide
spectrum of influence between those two extremes, of course. How does
it look to you?

9. In relation to God, what do you think about yourself?

 Simply the idea of standing beside God can be intimidating to some
people, leading them to respond about how they look at themselves as
being very small. Others think that being beside God is the most natural
state in the world. What is true for you?

10. In relation to God, how do you feel about yourself?

 Is it shame and guilt, or love and self-acceptance? Perhaps a feeling
such as sadness shows up and you don't see a direct association with
God.

11. In relation to God, how do you behave toward yourself?

 Some people say that being with God stirs a desire to make dramatic
changes in their lives including deepening their faith and connection with
God.

12. How does the way that you think, feel, and behave toward yourself in
relation to God impact your life and others' lives?

 Your response may reaffirm the value of your belief in God and how
you practice that belief, or it may trigger memories of how you have felt
unfulfilled in this arena.

Before you begin to track your emotional statements, remember the atheist who raged about God allowing all the suffering in the world? He was willing to explore this anger, even if it was unexpected as a response to being asked about God. He didn't connect with any childhood memories of feeling angry about unfair conditions, but he did spend time simply being present with that emotion. He happened to have chosen politics as a career, so he was actively engaged in trying to improve human conditions. But when he completed his moment of being with his emotions, he reported a different attitude toward the work he was doing. He saw more clearly the power and influence he had, what he could actually do for humanity, and what he could let go of trying to do.

Now it's time for you to discover what lies behind your declarations and feelings about God. If you have a strong negative core belief to uncover, simply go to appendix A for the full exercise.

BEING WITH DEATH

As you approach the last life area of your Awareness Integration journey, you are going to come face-to-face with death. Well, that's a frightening thought, isn't it? It is for most people. Others accept that the experience of dying is both inevitable and a natural part of life. At this stop you will have the opportunity to explore your own personal concepts of death and your reactions to considering the prospect of your own death, whenever it may come. Let me first assure you that for most of my clients who have worked with this model, this life area has been a valuable and often intriguing visit—even if they did begin with just a little anxiety.

For now, our focus is on being with the idea of death. Before we look at some of the helpful guideposts that can help prepare you for this exploration, I'd like you to follow a simple exercise, which is shaped by answering two questions:

1. When do you think you are going to die?

   If you first answer by writing "I have no idea," I urge you to go on and calculate some sort of estimate, based on your family history, your current health, and other relevant factors. Then you may arrive at some age: eighty, eighty-five, ninety, or something much earlier. It's just a guess, not a sentence!

2. If you died tomorrow, what would you have fulfilled in your life and what, if anything, would be left unfulfilled?

   Spend a few moments taking inventory of what fits in those two categories. Then look back at your answer to your first question. Note how many years you have projected you have left. Is it twenty years, thirty years, or even longer? That means you have time left to fulfill more of what you hope to materialize in your life. You've already made a potentially useful self-discovery shaped by one consideration of death, and you have not yet even plunged into the core questions of Awareness Integration as they relate to this life area. As you look at what would be incomplete, brainstorm ideas of what you would need to do or say to those in your life in order to feel complete.

As you proceed with the questions, you may observe that your reflections touch upon these four aspects of death: (1) the form of death you anticipate and the act of dying itself; (2) the sense of loss you are apt to experience from imagining the end to your life; (3) an evaluation of your life, going beyond what was fulfilled and unfilled and extending into a full review of how you lived; and (4) a reference to your beliefs about an afterlife.

Your answers may sound mostly abstract, or they may pull in the spiritual depths. There is no right or wrong way to be with death in this manner. It's just your own experience.

It's possible that as you first think about death, feelings of loss will be triggered related to loved ones who have died. What do you most vividly remember about your relationship with that person or a beloved pet that died? How did your life change because of that death?

In your evaluation of your life, do you find yourself being judged—clearly destined for hell or heaven? Or is it a more personal assessment of what you've done and how you've lived? Do you accept your achievements and your failures, or do you blame yourself, or others, for what didn't happen?

Do you experience anger when noting a belief such as "when you're dead, you're dead" because you don't believe in any kind of afterlife? Or do you firmly believe that we have a spirit and hold a sweet image of afterlife that enables you to approach the idea of your death with a greater sense of peace? When I have answered these questions for myself, I found myself declaring, "I am not coming back." That conclusion is not based on any particular spiritual belief; it's simply my imagination. Your imagination will likewise steer your responses. I have had clients vowing that they would come back in the next life just to get their revenge on those who wronged them in this life!

As you consider the manner in which your death may come, do you find yourself hoping that you won't have to suffer through some terminal illness or disability? Death is one thing we have no control over, but we can still wish it will happen one way rather than another way.

Open yourself to what you will discover now as you gently and respectfully imagine yourself being with death.

1. What do you think of death?

    Your answers may cover general concepts about what death is and what it isn't. It's also possible that your responses will focus on what you think about your own death. Follow your own trail.

2. How do you feel about death?

    Would you say, "I am scared of death because it's the only thing I am powerless against" or "I invite death since I feel free"?

3. How do you behave toward death?

    Do you accept it, rebel against it, or pretend it doesn't exist? In your life, would you say you have moved toward death or away from it? Have you ever challenged death, perhaps by engaging in risky behavior? Have you survived your possible death?

4. How does the way you think, feel, and behave toward death impact your life and others' lives?

    Have you obsessed about death in ways that others say are unhealthy? Does a fear of death cause you anxiety that shows up in many other contexts?

5. When you imagine yourself facing death, what do you think about yourself?

    Do you think about what's going to happen next in relation to a possible afterlife? Do you think mostly about how well you lived your life? Or do you think about something else entirely?

6. When you imagine yourself facing death, how do you feel about yourself?

    Perhaps you feel grateful for the life you have lived or sad and disappointed that you will not be there for those you care most about. Is there a degree of pride in yourself or regret laced with sadness? See where your feelings take you.

7. When you imagine yourself facing death, how do you behave toward yourself?

    Do you suddenly wish you had not beaten yourself up for specific acts while you were alive because, on balance, you know you did the best you could? Is there compassion for yourself or a degree of blame?

8. How does the way you think, feel, and behave toward yourself when you imagine yourself facing death impact your life and others' lives?

    Perhaps you do sometimes think about death in your day-to-day life. If so, what has been the effect of such experiences? Have your thoughts and feelings about yourself that spring from fixating on death limited you in any way? Have they inspired you?

As you have been doing with the other life areas, identify those statements and concepts that seem to point to a negative core belief. What self-assessment has a real charge as you repeat it? Something such as "I've wasted half my life" would suggest the presence of an associated emotion and negative core belief. Find your starting place for this part of the visit with death now by going to appendix A for the full exercise. Look at what needs to be complete in your life so you can live the rest of life as new every day.

You are going to roll right into the next important phase of your Awareness Integration experience: the return journey through the seven life areas you have just covered. The next chapter will walk you through this exciting and pivotal process.

Chapter Nine

With a Free Mind and a Heart of Love

The Awareness Integration Return Journey

In the last part of your Awareness Integration journey, you imagined that you were coming face-to-face with your own death. So what happens next? You now have the opportunity to imagine that you are coming back to life. Or, if you do not relate to the sense of having literally encountered death, you can simply remind yourself that you are still very much alive. You still have time. You have time to fulfill what has been unfulfilled and time to live in the spirit and attitude more in alignment with your deepest values and your most passionate goals.

In a way, you really will have the chance to hit the Life Reset button as you embark on the Awareness Integration return journey. In this process, you will revisit the same seven life areas you just followed, but you will be doing so with a very different approach and a fresh mindset. You will be applying what you have learned on the first phase of the journey to actively reevaluate how you would like to think, feel, and behave in all those realms of life.

The work that you will be doing on this return journey will serve as a solid foundation for becoming more accountable for your life and for actualizing the goals and intentions that mean the most to you. You may find that your experience feels like a spiritual rebirth, or it may be more of a mental and emotional exercise. Either way, my hope is that when you complete this return journey, you will come away with a stronger belief that you truly deserve to be happy, have more of what you want, and experience greater freedom to take you where you heart yearns to go.

Before you set sail on this leg of the journey, you will need some fresh supplies. As well as pulling together the insights and healing that the Awareness Integration process has already yielded, you will be spending a few moments here answering some very important questions. So get out your journal, flip on your recording device, or reopen the app while trekking across the spectrum of those seven life areas, and reflect on the following inquiries:

Who do you want/intend to be? For example, do you want to be loving, curious, open, giving, or courageous?

What beliefs, concepts, or attitudes do you want/intend to adopt and follow? For example, perhaps you would say, "I am a co-creator of my life, and I will create great results as I put effort into them."

What emotions do you choose to feel (e.g., feelings such as joy, happiness, and gratitude)?

What values do you especially seek to live by? For example, do you want to be caring to all around you, to be accepting of people as they are, or to make a difference in people's lives?

Feel free to jot down as many notes as come to mind as you search for the statements that seem to most clearly, accurately, and affirmatively name your direction. You may say,

I intend to be loving.
I intend to live with honesty and integrity.
I intend to feel peaceful in my life, no matter what happens to me.
I intend to be compassionate.
I intend to treat people, and myself, with more kindness.
I intend to be a much healthier person.

Make a full and complete statement that captures the tone and feeling of who you really believe you are and who you want to be. It can be poetic or ethereal sounding, or it can sound as short and pithy as a bumper-sticker slogan. It's totally up to you. This is your return journey!

Your intention may reflect a desire to be more responsible for the choices that you make and how they impact you. Or maybe it will be to accept and forgive, rather than to judge and blame. Perhaps you seek to adopt a belief that much more is possible in life than you used to believe, or that you really can make a difference in the lives of others and the world around you.

Your values may include generosity, self-love, cherishing life, or telling the truth. Having a stronger faith may be surging to the front of your core values. Take all the time you need to sharpen the statements that seem to resonate most inside you. When I have escorted clients along the return journey, I have heard some moving statements about how they choose to live:

"I'm an embracing soul—loving, giving, and warm."
"I'm allowing every part of me to be free."
"I'm a light cleansed—solid and deserving."

Fara, who invested so much energy on the first part of the Awareness Integration journey as she cleansed deep emotions triggered by childhood abuse, said simply, "I am a strong woman." And that she was!

One way to look at this process of preparing for the return journey is that you are adopting a changed identity. Somehow or other, these new intentions, attitudes, and values are molding a picture that marks a significant difference from how you have been looking at yourself and how you have been living. Before you embarked on this journey of cultivating enhanced awareness of all the domains of your life, the identity that you had been operating under most likely came out of a limited and mostly unconscious way that you perceived yourself and the world around you. You made certain rigid decisions about yourself as an identity, and then related to other people and the world as that identity. Now you are shaping an identity from a much broader pool of understanding and intentionality. You are just so much more conscious of how you want to live.

This changed identity may look and feel totally new to you, or it may simply be a clearer and sharper image of who you are and where you are going. Keep in mind that you can make adjustments to this changed identity and your intentions and goals as you proceed along the return journey, as well as during the weeks and months ahead when you begin integrating these changes into your life.

So now picture yourself taking all these intentions and your sense of a changed identity and tucking them safely into your backpack. It's time to walk across the terrain of the Awareness Integration return journey. You will begin backtracking your steps by standing beside God or a higher being. Of course, if you are an atheist or otherwise do not relate to the concept of God or spirit, you may choose to skip ahead to the second set of questions related to who you want to be in the universe. Otherwise, take that primary guiding question of who you want to be and apply it specifically to your relationship with God now:

1. Who do you want to be in the presence of God/higher power/spirit?

    Do you hold different images about spiritual oneness? Do you feel God's grace and unconditional love and support drawing you forward toward actualizing your intentions? Whatever emerges, capture those expressions now.
2. What do you want to think in the presence of God? How do you want to feel in the presence of God? How do you want to behave in the presence of God?

    Your responses need not be long or complex. Stick to first thoughts and images: "I want to remember that my spiritual life really matters." "I want to feel more love and joy." "I want to nurture my relationship with God."

The last step of this process of revisiting the experience of standing beside God is to name any concrete goals that will be necessary or beneficial in meeting your intentions: "I will begin a meditation practice within the next two weeks." "I will go online this weekend and select a new book on spiritual practices." "I will find a church that's right for me."

Find the essence of what you most want to set out as your way of being with God in your life now. Allow any warmth or excitement that bubbles up to wash over you. You are doing something very positive for yourself, and your commitment is helping to usher in those affirming sensations.

TRACKING POSITIVE EMOTIONS

I will not be guiding you into a process of tracking painful or negative emotions as you revisit these life areas on your return journey, although you may need or want to do that occasionally when something troubling comes up. I'll say more about that in a moment. Generally, however, the mission in being present with your emotions has now changed, and you will be taking an entirely different approach.

Instead of choosing a charged emotion such as sadness, anger, or grief, you now get to choose one of the positive, life-enhancing emotions that naturally show up on this phase of the journey. And rather than watch how the intensity of this emotion goes down, you're going to track how it goes up—and even encourage its rise to full intensity.

Let's say you just experienced a sense of joy while you were imagining yourself in the presence of God. So joy is your emotion to track in this new way. Use the same questions you learned from being present with your emotions earlier during the first part of your journey:

Where do you experience this feeling in your body?
On a scale of zero to ten, what is the intensity of that feeling?

Close your eyes. Now, rather than search for a memory associated with this emotion, you are simply going to focus on this feeling in your body and let it soak in. Allow that sense of joy to permeate your entire body and being.

Next, bring back the number you initially assigned to reflect its intensity. Let's say it was a three. Fine, now I want you to raise that intensity of joy up to five. Breathe that in. See what it's like to let more joy in. Does it feel good? Is it something new for you? Great, but you're not done yet. Now I want you to raise the intensity of that joyful feeling all the way up to ten! If you were the optimum person you want to be, feeling all-out joy in this context, how would that be? Really register that sensation in your body. How amazing it is to do that!

Of course, there's no need to force this rising of intensity. But if it doesn't click initially, give it a second try. Pause, scan your body again, take a breath, and imagine that you are experiencing joy at the intensity level of ten. Call upon any other tools or resources you may know to build the resonance of a positive feeling.

Now open your eyes. Accept your experience, whatever it is. If you did sense that intensity level of your emotion rising, even if it didn't seem to reach a ten, take a moment to consider what you did to help build on that feeling. Was it deep breathing? Was it visualizing yourself acting in a joyful way around God or loved ones in your life? Was it placing your hands over your heart?

Whatever worked for you to encourage the fuller expression of that positive emotion is a skill that you can call upon as you experiment with tracking positive emotions throughout your return journey. Maybe it was a phrase that captures how you want to be in your life: "I am one with a loving God and so I bring love to all parts of my life." This skill that you just utilized in raising the intensity of a positive emotion is something that you can tap into for any challenging situation you encounter in your day-to-day life. If breathing deeply with your hands folded over your heart enabled you to increase the intensity of joy, you can do that whenever you'd like to feel more joy.

You can also call upon this skill when you simply would like to come back to your main intention of how you want to be (e.g., "I want to be loving and compassionate") during a moment when something comes up that tests your ability to hold to that intention. You simply take a deep breath, fold your hands over your heart (or whatever skill you choose), and repeat again, "I want to be loving and compassionate." By raising the intensity level of that intention, you enhance your ability to actualize that mode of being in dealing with the difficult person or conflict in front of you.

Let's say you are driving in your car and someone cuts you off. Rather than flipping them the bird, you can call in that intention of being loving and compassionate. I live and drive in Southern California, where all of us are tested on this front often. Sometimes it takes the example of others from far away to remind us of our positive intention. Once, while I was traveling in the South, a woman driving beside me pulled down her window and invited me to do the same. "If I am ever in your way again, just let me know. Thank you," she said. I got it—I had been driving in a noncourteous way, no doubt due to my Southern California influence. This woman let me know that in the gentlest, compassionate way you could imagine. She didn't even honk. It was total love and acceptance. Even if she was telling me off sarcastically, her way of delivering it with love made me be more responsible about my lack of attentiveness toward others. I imagined that she was living by her own intention to relate to others in that spirit.

You will have that opportunity to actualize your intentions, whatever they may be, every day.

Now imagine yourself picking up your backpack again and moving on to the next life area.

NATURE AND THE UNIVERSE

Who do you want to be in nature and the universe?
How do you want to think, feel, and act toward nature and the universe?

Maybe you want to be more connected to everything around you, rather than just being a separate and insignificant speck in the universe. If your guiding intention is to be more loving, what does it mean to you to be more loving toward the universe? Follow your thoughts and feelings wherever they go, even if they no longer seem to directly relate to the concept of being in the universe. You're simply bringing greater awareness into how you will live your life.

If you have any specific goals that seem to fit this stop, include those now. If there is a positive emotion you would like to be present with, and consciously shift it to a higher intensity, feel free to do so. However, you do not need to stop to be present with a specific positive emotion at each stage of this return journey. You will know when it is the right time to do so. If none calls out to you here, move right along to the next life area.

If your desire in life is to be more compassionate, how will that translate to your relationship with nature? Will you make a vow, as I did not long ago, not to kill another living thing—including those pesky insects and bugs that invade your home? Or is there a particular goal that will reflect your desire to be more engaged in life around you, perhaps joining a cause to save our oceans and all the sea creatures that live there from pollution?

YOUR IDENTITY

Now the return journey gets more personal. Imagine yourself back in that tunnel of mirrors, with mirrors all around you. Or bring back that physical mirror that you used for the life area of being with yourself while looking in the mirror.

Who do you want to be with yourself?
How do you want to think, feel, and act toward yourself?
What specific goals will be helpful in actualizing your intentions?

Again, your initial responses may stem from a physical image. If you want to adopt an attitude of living in a healthier way, you want to feel more energy, or you want to be more nurturing, what will that mean? Look for concrete goals to set you on the right course. Does part of the picture of your healthier life include losing weight? If so, what will you do to make that happen? Perhaps you will exercise twice a week. If you want to look and feel better, maybe you will eliminate sugar and carbs from your diet.

Carefully consider which goals will bring you closer to who and what you want to be on the physical realm. Then reflect on the more emotional dimension of being with yourself while looking at your reflection in the mirror. Here you might name an intention to be kinder toward yourself and to feel more nurtured. Does that mean committing to a nightly bath, getting your hair done once a week, or finally investing in a pedicure? Write down those goals that will support your mission.

If you proclaim that you want to be more forgiving of yourself, what steps do you want to take when you realize that you have done something wrong? Perhaps it will be to tell yourself something like, "I made a mistake, but it's okay and I'm ready to go forward" rather than "I am so stupid!"

In this close-up look at yourself, don't be surprised if feelings and core beliefs you dealt with during your first time through the Awareness Integration journey reemerge. It's natural for old residue to get stirred up when you face yourself in the mirror on the return journey. For some of my clients, the minute they hit the tunnel of mirrors, unresolved issues fly back up in their face. You may be telling yourself that "I am kind and loving," but if you have not cleared out all the major emotions that get in the way of that changed identity, you won't believe it deep inside. That's the wall you hit in this tunnel of mirrors. Even if you believed you had released all your influential charged emotions when you tracked your feelings on the first phase of the journey, you may have missed some.

You have the opportunity to clean up that old residue right now. As I mentioned a few moments ago when I introduced the new tool of tracking and amplifying positive emotions in this phase of your journey, you are likely to encounter a situation now and then when you want and need to revisit the process of tracking the more charged or negative emotions that crop up. So if your harsh voice declares that you are "selfish" or "unloving," take that negative concept that seems to be blocking your way from realizing your new intention to be kind and loving toward yourself and track it now. Follow the same procedure of naming the feeling, locating it in your body, identifying the intensity, and closing your eyes to invite an associated memory. Then see if you can facilitate a releasing of the charge. I trust that you can utilize that important tool when necessary.

If you do track any charged emotion here, stay with it until it's complete. Then return to the primary question: Who do I want to be toward myself right now? And cut yourself some slack. Sometimes clients working in this area of the return journey notice that they have consistently been living with an ingrained habit such as emotionally beating themselves up. It's what they have known all their lives, and it's not going away at the snap of a finger. So they experience a degree of sadness, shake their heads, and mutter, "I'm just a depressed person." Then I remind them that sadness is just a human emotion, and having a moment of feeling sad does not mean you are depressed. Note the sadness, and work with it as you need to, but also pay attention to other emotions you are experiencing, especially if they feel new or more pronounced. If you notice a persistent state of depression, seek professional help.

Of course, you may be noticing that looking at yourself in the mirror actually fuels positive emotions. Daniel, who was working on low self-confidence around women as he made his way across the Awareness Integration terrain the first time, noticed right away that he felt calmer while looking at himself in the mirror than he did the first time. "I feel kind of taller now, too," he beamed.

What kinds of changes are you experiencing?

SETTING AND ACHIEVING GOALS

As you get ready to leave the mirror and move along the Awareness Integration return journey, bear in mind that the process of naming goals and taking concrete action steps to achieve them will become more and more central to your process of making positive change in your life. To help you maximize that process, let's spend a moment clarifying what goals are and what they aren't.

First, it's helpful to distinguish a goal from a fantasy or dream. A fantasy is something that sounds nice or even euphoric, but it's not something you think will ever actually happen. Sure, it would be nice to have wings and fly, but that "goal" is not so realistic, is it? It is more of an imaginary concept to make you feel good. A dream may seem like a goal because it does at least sound possible, but you have no action plan to take the steps to achieve it. You can say, "I am going to be a millionaire," but then you have to ask yourself, how am I going to become a millionaire? What is my plan to bring such an influx of money in my life? What am I going to do, and when am I going to do it? Without taking those concrete steps, your goal remains a dream.

So how can you tell whether something you are naming as a goal to bring more positive change in your life is really a viable goal that you can work toward? In many circles of life coaching and other therapeutic resources for helping people make positive changes, the use of this acronym has been helpful:

S   specific
M   measureable
A   attainable/assignable
R   realistic
T   time related

In other words, your goals should reflect a specific outcome that is tangible and lends itself to concrete action steps to make it happen. Let's say you establish the general goal we mentioned earlier of living a healthier lifestyle. You begin to make that tangible by setting the measureable goal of exercising twice a week or eliminating sugar from your diet. This is a maintenance goal, meaning that the goal itself is ongoing and your process of monitoring it is also ongoing. So you can ask yourself, Did I exercise twice last week? Did I exercise twice this week? At the end of each week, can you look back and say you exercised twice that week as well?

Some goals that you establish will be long term: "In the next ten years I will visit thirty different countries all over the world." That only becomes a measureable goal when the ten years are up, but to help make sure this doesn't become a dream, you bolster it with short-term goals: "by the end of next year, I will visit one country."

The key advantage of setting these kinds of tangible, attainable goals is to strengthen the likelihood that what you envision and desire will actually happen. When you name and schedule what you're going to do to achieve the goal you want, you counterbalance one of those basic realities about living in today's world: Either you create your own schedule or life will give you one. In other words, create the schedule that includes the checkpoints related to your goal so things won't keep coming up to sabotage or derail you.

When you take the time to set up goals all along this return journey of your Awareness Integration experience, you can also witness and appreciate the growth that is emerging in your life. Establishing goals and then achieving them add to your self-confidence. You just start feeling better. At the end of each month, and then each year, you can look at what you have achieved. Being able to say, "I declared it and it came true!" gives you a tremendous sense of power.

Watching my clients achieve their goals is an especially rewarding experience for me in working with the Awareness Integration Model. Feeling fulfilled and achieving what you want is one of the primary goals of Awareness Integration.

One important component of the process of setting and achieving goals is to recognize the critical need of establishing a concrete action plan for each and every goal. What are the tangible steps you will need to take, and when and how will you take them in order to get to the new place you wish to be? Without an action plan, your goal can remain something too far "out there" rather than something real that you are marching toward via a specific course of action. I recommend that you formulate these action plans for every goal that you establish at each life area you revisit during this phase of the Awareness Integration journey.

So let's get back on the trail of this return journey so you can continue to name how you want to be in all the other life areas, and you can keep setting meaningful goals to help you fulfill your mission and step into this changed identity. You need not stop at each and every life area. Some may not apply to you in going forward in your life. If your parents are deceased, for example, you may decide to bypass the life areas focused on your relationships with them. And if you do not have children, you can jump over that life area as well.

Some life areas will be well suited to working with as a group or block during this phase of the journey. This will become clear to you as you go forward.

LOVE

Who do you want to be in the presence of love?
How do you want to think, feel, and act toward love?
What specific goals will be helpful in actualizing your intentions?
What is the concrete action plan that will set you on the right course and keep
    you on it?

Because this is one of the intangible life areas, in contrast to those life areas that zero in on your relationships with people in your life, you may not have major revelations here, especially if love is already addressed in your guiding intentions of who you want to be as you move through this return journey. However, some important insight or feeling may come up. If it does, by all means make note of it.

Who do you want to be toward any illness, disability, or addiction you face in life? How do you want to think, feel, and act toward those physical, mental, or emotional challenges?

What specific goals will be helpful in actualizing your intentions?
What is the concrete action plan that will set you on the right course and keep
    you on it?

If you have been wrestling with any kind of addiction, this is certainly a good opportunity to assert those clear, tangible goals: getting back to AA or NA meetings twice a week, seeing an addictions counselor or therapist once a week, obtaining a new resource book on recovery, and so forth. If you are working with a physical challenge, and your overall intention is to be healthier in every way, perhaps a new approach in relating to your condition now is to commit to joining a support group for those living with the same challenge. Or maybe you schedule an appointment for physical therapy. If you note that you want to be more loving toward yourself, maybe that means adopting a more accepting attitude toward your physical or mental condition. What specific goals might help you demonstrate that commitment?

PARENTS

Who do you want to be in your relationship with your parents or other care-
    givers?
How do you want to think, feel, and act toward your parents or caregivers?
What specific goals will be helpful in actualizing your intentions?
What is the concrete action plan that will set you on the right course and keep
    you on it?

For some of you, this stop may not apply, although if your parents are deceased you may want to briefly consider these questions as they relate to the
feelings you still have toward your mother and father and the attitude you
want to carry about their influence on your life.

For those still engaged with one or both parental relationships, this may
be an especially fruitful stop on the return journey. You may be pointing
your compass toward a very new and different way of relating to your
mother or father, so your willingness to slow down and carefully explore
your intentions, thoughts, feelings, behaviors, and goals will be especially
important.

Let's say your guiding intention is to be loving toward your mother,
something you struggle to do with any consistency amidst the conflicts and
challenges that arise. Good for you for believing that a new course is even
possible! Now, try to flesh out what it means. Perhaps it means that you want
to have clear communication with her. Maybe you want her to know that you
love and appreciate her. Or you wish to be more accepting of who she is and
how she behaves toward you, toward herself, or toward the world around her.

How do you want to feel toward your mother? Is it simply love? Maybe
gratitude is another one of your desired emotions? How do you want to act?

Maybe you simply want to behave in a more caring and consistent way. Well, tangible goals will help ground that intention. Perhaps you commit to calling her every Saturday.

The idea is to bring this "loving" intention fully into how you will think, feel, and act toward your mother. That's what this return journey of Awareness Integration is all about: living by your intention in every realm of life and every context of how you live. Is that going to be challenging? Of course it will. All growth and change come with challenges. But is it also going to be exciting? I trust that you already have felt your own excitement rising.

Let's further examine this intention of being more loving with your mother. Perhaps, when you first journeyed across the Awareness Integration trail and spent time looking at your relationship with your mother, you noted how you often feel aloof toward her. So in addition to wanting to be loving, you might now commit to being more connected. Calling once a week will help, and perhaps you also want to commit to a structure of spending time with her. One client I worked with decided to set a goal of taking an overnight trip with her mother within the next three months.

You will also benefit from choosing the quality of interaction you have with your mother when you do talk to her and see her. Perhaps your intention will be to accept who she is, which means not saying critical or judgmental things, and not getting "hooked" if she criticizes you! You can say to yourself, "I don't like those particular qualities in her, but I still love her as my mother." Then you can adopt strategies to avoid those moments when you feel a charge toward her and are tempted to rush in with a negative response.

If you have been focusing at first on your intention of being with your mother, now is the time to also fully consider how you want to be with your father. After gaining all the awareness that has come to you about this core relationship, how do you now want to think about your father? How do you want to feel about him? How do you want to act toward him?

Perhaps it has been difficult for you to cultivate the kind of connection that you might like to have with your father for many years. Now, with your core sense of how you want to be in your life, the door may open to a new approach, a fresh perspective, and a different way of carrying yourself. You will know what that is and how to explore the new possibilities.

Sometimes having the goal to live by intentions such as these requires adopting new skills. A therapist or life coach can assist you with how to follow your desired new way of being with your mother or father. Just as you may have needed a therapist on the first phase of the journey when emotional issues became overwhelming, you may want to call upon a therapist or life coach now to learn new skills and better navigate the obstacles that show up.

This may be an excellent time to focus on a particular positive emotion that comes from naming your intention and sensing how it will feel to put it in motion. Is there a sense of excitement? Track that feeling, or any positive emotion that is present, and take that extra step of bringing it up to an intensity level of ten. It just feels good to know that you are in the process of behaving in a life-affirming way.

SIGNIFICANT OTHER

Who do you want to be in your relationship with your spouse or mate?
How do you want to think, feel, and act toward your spouse or mate?
What specific goals will be helpful in actualizing your intentions?
What is the concrete action plan that will set you on the right course and keep
   you on it?

If you are married or in a committed relationship, you're likely to feel a lot of "juice" in your stop here on your return journey. In contrast to your parents, where your contact may not be on a daily basis, your spouse is right there in your life all the time. So you will have ample opportunities every day to try to live by your new intended way of being in this relationship.

Do your best to flesh out the picture of just how you want to engage in this connection. If you want to be more loving, note that. If you want to share passionate sex, and more often, by all means include that. If you seek more fun in general, add that to your intentions. If you want to feel more relaxed in your relationship instead of being so anxious about it, spell that out too. If part of your answer to how you want to act toward your spouse is communicating more clearly, that will also be an important part of your desired picture.

Write or speak all these responses. Then, when you feel complete with this life area, here's the next important step: Share it with your spouse. Even if your spouse has not been actively involved in or fully aware of your work with Awareness Integration to this point, now's the time to change that. Explain to your spouse the idea behind the return journey and the specifics of what you have been exploring in this life area. Extend a sincere request to get on board together now.

As a couple, your first assignment is this: create a relationship mission statement. In other words, you are adjusting the question of "how do I want to be in my relationship" to "how do we want to be in our relationship?"

Once you have something you can both agree on and feel good about it, write it down and hang it on your bedroom wall, mirror, or some other prominent and visual place in your home. Make sure you get clear on how you both define important reference points. If you say you want more trust in your relationship, how do you define trust? Then brainstorm together on goals to help make this mission statement a reality. Do you want to commit to a date night where you get all dressed up once a week, or do you want to schedule some fun activity to engage in together regularly? Perhaps it will help to spend two hours each week just sitting and talking, so that any relationship issues that have arisen, especially those that threaten your mission statement, can be addressed before they fester.

There are many other tangible goals you can consider. Looking over a self-help relationship guidebook may provide you with more ideas. One tool I have found very effective in my work with couples is for both of you to begin each morning by saying to the other person, "I choose you today."

Getting your spouse on board will certainly make your new attitudes, intentions, and goals in this life area more real and engaging. The work you do here will also help you take your desired changes into other relationships in your life, including your relationship to work and career. You will have more ideas to draw from, and the energy that stems from enhancing your primary relationship can't help but add more momentum to other life changes.

Now, if you are not currently married or in what you consider a significant relationship, does that mean you automatically pass on this life area? Well, if you don't want a relationship, perhaps because you have reached a stage in your life when it is no longer an important goal, sure, move on to the next life areas of the return journey. However, if you are single and looking, this is your chance to give voice to what type of relationship you want.

When I work with clients seeking to attract a fulfilling intimate relationship, I instruct them to devise a one-hundred-item list that describes their ideal mate and ideal relationship. Why one hundred? Because if I just told them to "make a list," the entries would tend to be automatic or clichéd. So I say, "Fine, you can start with those automatic responses, but then you need to dig a little deeper." Often they will come back with a list of twenty-five items to capture their ideal mate. "Great," I say, "now add seventy-five more." When they make a face, I add, "This is the growth area for you. Look at the example of others in positive relationships. Read self-help books or romance novels, or watch romantic movies. You can find more."

Most clients stick with the task until their list is complete. Then, when they go on a date, the mission is to evaluate this potential mate according to that list. Even getting someone up to an 80–90 percent or a B on this grading scale can feel like a major step up in the process of seeking a healthy relationship. Now, if you are single and do compile such a list, remember that you have to meet the criteria too. If you name "honesty" as one important character trait in a partner, then you have to be honest too.

I've given you a lot to do in this stop of your return journey. These changes probably won't happen all at once, but if you are sincere in your intentions, and you build a list of tangible goals to support your efforts, you are well on your way to important change. That lab work of actualizing those changes will be ongoing. In the meantime, let's continue along the path of the Awareness Integration return journey.

CHILDREN

Who do you want to be in your relationship with your children?
How do you want to think, feel, and act toward your children?
What specific goals will be helpful in actualizing your intentions?
What is the concrete action plan that will set you on the right course and keep you on it?

If you do not have children, use this section to talk instead about your relationship with your pet, or you may jump to the next stop of naming who you want to be in your relationship with your siblings and other family members. But if you are a parent, you are likely to find that bringing more life-affirming intentions and positive emotions to your way of being with your children will pay major dividends. Most of us tend to judge ourselves harshly as parents, so tapping new values and attitudes toward this responsibility can serve to breathe renewed life into our efforts. If you are working on being more forgiving of both your children and yourself, then you may choose to write down all those specific things that your children did that you need to forgive them for, as well as all those things you did "wrong" in parenting that you wish to forgive yourself for.

Be as clear as you can about your goals and the action steps needed to stick to them. If you want to be more patient with your children, what will you do to back that up when your patience is tested? If you want to let them know how much you respect them, what can you do to display that respect? Also, don't forget that your intentions and goals may be slightly different for each child. Construct your responses accordingly.

If you find yourself infused with a deeper love for your children in this visit on your return journey, you could certainly benefit from stopping to be with

that love and seeking to increase the intensity of this feeling to ten. I suggest
for you to complete the list for each child.

FAMILY MEMBERS

Who do you want to be in your relationship with your siblings, your in-laws,
  or other family members in your life?
How do you want to think, feel, and act toward your siblings, in-laws, and
  other family members in your life?
What specific goals will be helpful in actualizing your intentions?
What is the concrete action plan that will set you on the right course and keep
  you on it?

As you think about adopting a changed identity, one that may look very new
to family members who have known you for many years, how would you like
it to turn out? Ideally, of course, all these people who know you will heap
piles of praise and appreciation for your way of being more loving, kind, or
patient around them. Well, that certainly could happen. It also may turn out
that they hardly notice the change in you at all. Are you prepared to hold to
your new commitment even if you do not receive that external validation
from others? As part of naming goals in this area, it will help to include
what you will do if one or more siblings fail to recognize any change in your
behavior and does not change anything about how they act toward you. If
the same conflict seems to be hanging in the air, perhaps you will choose to
set new boundaries to break the old patterns. Or maybe you have a different
solution in mind that you can commit to as a goal.

  In approaching this life area, it will again be helpful to ask the core questions for each individual family member. And if you're serious about making
meaningful changes in these relationships, you will probably want to start
with the sibling or family member who presents the greatest challenge. This
is where your growth will come.

  Keep in mind the part about making a goal that is realistic. If you have
struggled through thirty years of conflict with your older sister, it's not very
realistic to imagine that all that conflict will simply melt away and transform
into one big ball of love, is it? It may be more realistic to name as your goal
your commitment not to make angry, judgmental remarks to her when she
acts that way toward you. You may simply choose silence as a way to align
with your intention to be more peaceful in your life and in all your relationships. Remember too that your initial strategies may not work to achieve the

goals you set for yourself. That's okay. You can simply shift your strategies. You're in this for the long haul.

A FASTER PACE

Have you noticed how this return journey moves along much faster than the first round of visits with the seven life areas? This is natural because you have a more focused and specific purpose now. Rather than taking a broad inventory of thoughts, feelings, and behavior, you are starting with a pronounced way of being and trying that on for the various life areas. How does your changed identity fit in the context of your relationships with other people and life around you? What are your intended thoughts, feelings, and behavior associated with those life areas, and what goals will support those desired results? You know exactly what you're up to as you proceed on this return journey, and you're taking many life areas together in blocks.

More than having this specific mission, though, your pace is faster because, more than likely, you have a sense of momentum building as you proceed along the return journey. Isn't it fun, or exciting, or simply new to look at your life in all those dimensions through the lens of a changed identity? Instead of problems, you are seeing possibilities. Rather than the same constant struggles you have known, you imagine a greater ease and freedom. Walls may be tumbling down.

As you brainstorm how you will think in these life areas, you may be identifying new core values that will serve as markers on your new course: integrity, courage, and perseverance. In considering how you feel, you may be noticing an accumulation of positive emotions, including some that may surprise you: exhilaration, pure acceptance, unconditional love, and pride. As you name your intended behavior at each stop, you may be heartened to point to such descriptions as caring, expressive, or responsible. It's fun and exciting to uncover the depths of a changed identity, isn't it? It naturally propels you forward when you find more ways, in more different contexts, of being the person you feel you really can be.

So keep your momentum going! Move through these life areas at the pace that feels right for you. Just make sure to be clear about your intended ways of being, and spend the time needed to articulate your goals that will help make that happen. Those goals, of course, can always be adjusted later. Things will change. Obstacles will come up. But for now, the idea is to breathe fully into this vision of how it can be, and claim it with your full being.

CAREER AND MONEY

Who do you want to be in your relationship with your work, career, and
  money?
How do you want to think, feel, and act toward your work, career, and
  money?
What specific goals will be helpful in actualizing your intentions?
What is the concrete action plan that will set you on the right course and keep
  you on it?

So what values do you want to hold in this realm? Do you imagine success
and prosperity? Okay then, which emotion do you want to experience, excitement or joy? And how do you want to act? Do you want to communicate responsibly, maintain integrity, and so forth? Now set the goals that will make
this vision tangible to you. Name the salary you want to make, and when, or
a position or title you want to hold. Set reasonable short- and long-term goals
with realistic timelines, backed with clear action plans. And don't be afraid to
embrace any goal or vision, from founder of your own billion-dollar company
to happy and fulfilled stay-at-home mom or dad.

This may be a good time to consider again whether you are really living
your passion with your work. If you have not actualized your dream job or
career, what steps do you need to take, right now, to start moving in that direction? It may help to review your notes from your first stop at this life area
on the Awareness Integration journey. You may have talked about a desired
change in your work for years, but now it's time to finally act. You have a
changed identity to live by! Of course, if you know that realistically you need
to stick with a job that is not absolutely ideal for now, you can consider how
you can bring in more of your newly claimed values and your deeper passion
into doing the work you're actually doing.

Don't forget to give voice to your intention in dealing with bosses, coworkers, and colleagues. How do you want to think, feel, and act toward those
relationships? Is there one person in particular that needs your attention in
actualizing your new approach?

FRIENDS AND OTHER PEOPLE

Who do you want to be in your relationships with your friends, acquaintances, and other people around you in the world?
How do you want to think, feel, and act toward your friends, acquaintances,
  and other people around you in the world?

What specific goals will be helpful in actualizing your intentions?
What is the concrete action plan that will set you on the right course and keep you on it?

You may want to take an individual approach in naming how you want to be with one or more specific friends or people you deal with on a regular basis. It does not have to be a "problem" relationship either. Maybe you have a friend whom you could become closer to, because doing so would fit your changed identity and the values and goals that you have been pointing to throughout your return journey. Or perhaps there is a new friend whom you wish would reach out to you now.

With existing relationships, if you carry the overriding commitment to be self-nurturing, perhaps that signals a freedom from having to please other people out of a sense of obligation. You get to choose how you actually want to be in relation to others. That is the beauty of the growth that emerges from Awareness Integration.

In this category, you need not limit yourself to how you will think, feel, and act toward people. You can expand your horizons to bring in how you want to engage with the rest of the world, to claim your place in it. As you gain more confidence and commitment, you may come to recognize that you actually have more power to influence so much of what's around you.

Maybe you'll choose to join a local, regional, national, or global cause that aligns with your values. Or maybe you'll launch some new cause, group, or organization. Your voice has power; how can you use it? Perhaps you will want to begin with the community that you know and then extend out to those you don't know.

I urge you not to fail to realize your greatness, wherever you are and whatever you do. It is your life. You really do have choices about how to direct it, how to react to it, and how to feel about what is happening to you. It's important to accept yourself for the choices that you've been making in your life, but it's even more important to accept the concept that you really do get to choose what you have to a much greater degree than you may have imagined. You actually can choose your emotions, rather than simply having them come upon you due to circumstance. Setting up a conscious choice about how we will live enables us to more consistently choose and experience those emotions that we want.

Your return journey is no doubt helping you to move further and further from a place of being a victim or feeling powerless to change what's around you. You can challenge yourself to wake up every morning and realize that you have chosen and continue to choose what you have in life. Taking responsibility for your choices is a big part of what elevates your life experience.

The intentions, values, and attitudes that you have been claiming during this part of the Awareness Integration experience will help you to grasp this way of approaching life.

You are closing in on the finish line of your return journey. How does it feel to have reached this point? Give yourself credit for what your new awareness has brought to you, and soak in the beauty and strength of your new intentions, values, and goals. There's just one more step to complete this return journey.

ANCHORING YOUR NEW ATTITUDES AND INTENTIONS

So now you've got a storehouse full of chosen values and more positive beliefs, emotions, and behaviors to apply to any life situation. You have been shaping a new identity to guide you through the kinds of changes that will bring you greater happiness and fulfillment. You've been constructing the tangible goals and the concrete action plans that will help put a structure to your new directions. You've been busily writing, organizing, envisioning, and strategizing. Now, as you get ready for one last assignment, you get to relax your conscious mind and welcome in your more creative or intuitive side. You get to have some fun!

The task is to create a collage or some other visual image that will serve as a powerful visual reminder of who you want to be out in the world and where you intend to go. This visual creation is going to reinforce all of your chosen values, emotions, and behavior so that you can glance at it and remember the course you have set for yourself. It will be your anchor to help keep you solidly grounded during all kinds of weather that will arise as you move about your daily life.

Your anchor will enable you to keep in mind that you are in this for the long haul. The process of applying these important and exciting changes that you have been mapping out is not a one-time, black-and-white thing. It's a day-to-day commitment, and you can count on the world to keep putting things in front of you to test you. You say you want to be more loving? You are going to come face-to-face with people and situations that will make you want to growl and sharpen your fangs. You intend to be patient and as calm as the placid sea? Circumstances will swirl around you that seemed design to toss you into the churning waters. Is your changed identity one of greater strength? People will say or do things that are seemingly guaranteed to bring you to your knees. Do you choose to live with greater acceptance, moving away from the sadness that used to hold you back? You will likely find yourself waking up one morning with a sense of misery that makes sadness look good. You get to choose whether to stay stuck in that misery or reclaim your intention to accept what is.

Yes, you will be challenged big time. But what you have going for you after completing the Awareness Integration journey is an inner power constructed from the awareness that you have choices in life. You can summon that inner power to more consistently make the positive choices that will align you with your intended changes. Your collage will be a valuable tool in tapping that inner power.

You may have lots of experience in making collages, either as a simple artistic or creative expression or to help you process and enhance personal or spiritual growth exercises. It's also fine if this is a relatively new endeavor for you. The idea is to give yourself plenty of freedom to come up with the kind of expression that will speak to you. You may do some drawing or painting of your own. You may cut out pictures and images from magazines. If you like to do most things on your computer, you may choose to search the Internet to find just the right images to anchor your intended changes. Then start putting together what you have assembled in a free-flowing manner that somehow makes the statement you intend.

Before you begin your collage research, it will be helpful to do a little brainstorming to identify what you are most looking for. Using your journal or recording method, start by compiling a list related to these categories:

Values
Emotions
Behaviors

In each category, go back to your new goals and intentions for each life area that you just focused on during your return phase of the Awareness Integration journey. Jot down the key values, emotions, and behaviors that you named as being especially important to you as you seek to move in powerful new directions in your life. This will give you more tangible reference points as you select the visual symbols and representations to utilize in your collage.

It can be helpful to look for ways to amplify or exaggerate the feelings you wish to experience or live by. If you want to lose weight, the image of a beautiful and fit woman may be a strong incentive to follow your new intentions. If you want to capture joy, find something striking that really embodies utter joy. Some people resonate with role models selected from today's culture or from history. Make the kind of visual display that will make you think and feel in sync with your new way of being every time you glance at it. It's another profound way to highlight your life mission statement.

Use words to highlight the key ideas if you choose. Or maybe you don't need any words at all because the visual image speaks volumes by itself.

Your collage can play such an important part in actualizing your changes that I strongly encourage you to create more than one. In other words, do one primary collage that addresses the big picture of who and what you want to be. Then construct separate collages for each key life area that you focused on in charting your return journey along the Awareness Integration trail. So you have one collage that captures how you want to be in your relationship with your spouse, another one for your new approach to your work or career, and another one for how you will treat yourself. Do as many collages as it takes to enable you to feel complete with your visual representation. When I first practiced doing the Awareness Integration Model for myself, I covered an entire wall with 8.5" × 11" collages symbolizing the different aspects of my life.

Now, some of you may be saying, "I'm not a collage person. I need another way to do this." That's fine. Your mode of expression may be to select a singular symbol, some object that will capture an important value or feeling. So find symbols for love, happiness, courage, serenity, or whatever else ranks high on your list of core feelings or ways of being. Then display those symbols all around your house. Maybe you have in mind a stained-glass ornament or a ceramic bowl. It's okay to call upon the creative works of others to bring out the expressions that matter to you. Paintings, posters, or drawings may meet your needs, or maybe it's something as simple as a flag or banner.

If you have become more accustomed to expressing yourself through writing while doing your work with Awareness Integration, you can certainly build your expression primarily from words. Make your words and phrases big and bold, and allow yourself to be playful in how you bring those words together to make a significant statement.

Once you have constructed your collage or other representation, you need to find the right place to display it. Your bedroom may be an ideal location for your main collage, so you can see it before you go to sleep at night and when you get up in the morning. Other collages may fit well if placed close to this primary collage, or you may want to choose other locations in your home. You may be especially aware of your collage if you put it on your computer. If you have made an effective representation for who you want to be with work, bring that collage into your workplace and display it where it will hold your attention.

Some people who follow the Awareness Integration trail resonate with spoken words. You may be moved to take some of the key words from your notes on the return journey, and the words depicted or illustrated by your visual representation, and draft a simple guided meditation for yourself. Then you can record that meditation and play it for yourself after you have gotten comfortable and closed your eyes. Use those key adjectives and other descriptive words that get right to the heart of your desired change. Tailor the guided visualization to be all about you and the changes you seek.

When I arranged a brief meditation for Daniel, the young man working on a search for greater self-confidence around women and in all realms of his life, I invited him to imagine a light coming toward him that "represents confidence, comfort, competence, and relaxation" and that shined a pathway for him to "be you, have fun, engage effortlessly with everyone around you, knowing that you are solid inside."

Another guided meditation, this one for a client who had been noting her many dualities and was working to become aware of and balance them more effectively, included this passage:

> I accept and am proud of every part of myself. I have faith that with every part of myself integrated, I am free to choose what is best for me and what is best for people around me. I allow myself to let go of the thoughts, feelings, and behaviors that do not work for me, and I let go of being influenced by the thoughts, feelings, and behaviors of others that are not aligned with who I want to be. I promise to be attentive to the different parts of me and to the different ways I see reflected in anyone I come in contact with, whether I have a long-term relationship with that person or it's just a glance from someone who has come into my life for a millisecond. I remember that I am who I am and that I appreciate who I am.

You may seek out a counselor, therapist, or coach who has the right skills to assist you in devising some kind of guided meditation that will help ground you in your new intended ways of being in your life. It's simply one more possible tool to bring in.

PUT IT ALL INTO ACTION

After placing your collages or other visual representations of your changed identity and your intention to live by your chosen values and attitudes, I urge you to take out your calendar or day planner. Now refer back to the many detailed goals you outlined for actualizing your changes through all the life areas on your return journey. It's time to make those goals even more concrete. If you asserted that you will exercise two days per week, choose those days and write them into your calendar every week. If you and your spouse agreed that you will have a date night every Friday evening, mark down that commitment on every Friday of every week of every month. If you noted that you will more closely monitor your finances to build a stronger relationship with money, then choose the date each month when you will hold a financial meeting with yourself to track how you're doing.

Continue to bring all those action plans into the day-to-day reality of your calendar. Now, what about the skills that you noted as necessary to move you closer to a desired goal? If you're going to attend a class, find out when it starts and the day you need to register, and pencil that into your calendar. If you committed to consult a coach or advisor for some new skill or activity, circle the date by which you will have made your first appointment.

AN INTEGRATED LIFE

Your collages will be powerful allies for you as you seek to put all these changes into motion and practice them every day. Looking at them, touching them, and rearranging or adding to them will enable you to grasp the anchor that will help you hold onto your changed identity. Of course, you've still got to make it all happen.

As we mentioned at the start of this chapter, you will be tested regularly. Fortunately, you have resources and skills to assist you. You can look back at all the notes you gathered on your Awareness Integration return journey to remind yourself of your specific intentions, goals, values, and ways of being in diverse life circumstances. So, when some challenging situation emerges, you can stop and ask yourself this: Is my current behavior aligned with my new intentions? Am I speaking the words that will bring me closer to my stated way of being here? Is the emotion that I am holding onto one that will pull me forward? If your answer to any of these kinds of questions is "no," then you can frame the follow-up question: What adjustments do I need to make right now to get me back on course?

Let's say you intend to practice acceptance in your relationship with your husband. So you come home from a tough day hoping or even expecting that he will greet you with a warm embrace and empathetic words. Instead, he just mumbles a noncommittal "Hi" and continues with his own work assignment at his laptop. "Nice welcome," you say to yourself as you turn away. "And I bet I'm going to see that sour face the rest of the evening or longer." So you pout, and in response he pulls further away from you, and the chain reaction builds and lasts not only through the night but also over the next three days.

"Wait," you say to yourself, "I said I was going to practice acceptance." So the next time you get the mumbled "Hi," try accepting that he is reacting to something in his own life. You will feel calmer. "Is something bothering you?" you ask respectfully. Then he explains he just got a nasty e-mail that he needs to hunker down and respond to. His reaction had nothing to do with you at all. And as you accepted him for who he was, and even displayed a degree of empathy, he turns around and shows an interest in your day and your challenges of the moment. Your ability to pull your thoughts, feelings, and behavior into the sphere of your new intentions opens a door to a much better outcome.

A healthy, satisfying life is created when you are able to successfully integrate and align your thoughts, emotions, and behaviors with your intentions and desired way of being. The Awareness Integration Model is designed to help create a healthier, more fulfilled person, and that means bringing together those different components so that your intentions then serve as the magnet that pulls them together.

Thoughts, feelings, and behavior are all lining up at the door that opens to your commitment to be kind, accepting, loving, and generous in the world. Each part is just as important as the other parts. Your thoughts influence your feelings and behavior. Your feelings can trigger a thought or activate a behavior. Your behavior is critical because if you don't ultimately act in a way that's consistent with how you think and feel, your behavior is going to create an unintended result.

That's why this process of Awareness Integration focuses so consistently on these three realms. From start to finish, you have been addressing questions related to your thoughts, your feelings, and your behavior. At different points of the journey, you may have noticed the emphasis shifting from one of those realms to another. Early on in the journey you may have been doing more work on the cognitive level, gaining awareness of how you live. Then, when you began more regularly tracking your feelings and searching for the stories and the meaning behind them, your attention shifted to the emotional arena. Later, especially on the return journey, you have stated your goals in an action-oriented way. So the focus has been more on the behavioral part of your integrated life.

Now you are well positioned to build upon a foundation that incorporates integration, and you have the guiding skill of awareness to inform you when something is out of whack. So if fear comes up as you begin to actualize a chosen way of being, you can scan your awareness to see what message is coming through. Sometimes the act of seeing our intended change in black and white rather than on the colorful drawing board of our words or visual images can make it seem too hard to achieve. "I can never make it," you say to yourself, as you note a fear of failure or the residue from a past failure. You can work with that feeling and steer your intended thoughts and beliefs to encourage its release, to the point where it may yield to your intended feeling of excitement. The reality is that when living by a changed identity, it may often feel that you are riding on a balancing wire between fear and excitement.

Here's another idea to help you stick to the new course you have embarked on: Every night, write down one experience or event that promoted your most important values, whether it was something you acted out toward someone else or something that another person acted out toward you. Store that experience or event in a box or on a file in your computer to save for rainy days in your new way of being. So then if you find yourself in one of those days when you're feeling down in the dumps, discouraged about your ability to live by these new intentions, or struggling to value yourself and others, you can go to this box or file to remind yourself of all the love that is around you.

If you get overwhelmed in striving to achieve any of your goals, you might also find that your awareness steers into a recognition that you're simply trying to move too fast. Perhaps your expectations are a bit too high. You can take the time to reexamine your goals and identify whether one or more may really be a fantasy. That's okay. Simply ask yourself what would make that goal more realistic and adjust it accordingly. Remember, this is a lifestyle change. It's okay to make changes in how you are going to make change. The idea is to make a commitment, one that fills you with passion and purpose, and find the most successful and productive ways to feed that commitment.

Awareness Integration will be present with you every step of the way. It will always remind you that a more fulfilling life is very much possible and steer you in the direction that will make it a reality. Many blessings on your journey into a happier, healthier, more harmonious life!

Chapter Ten

The Journey Continues

This is an exciting time for those of us in a growing community who have tuned into the power and the possibilities of Awareness Integration. Professionally, I continue to receive an enthusiastic response when I present the model through workshops and seminars to conferences of professional therapists all across the country. I've been conducting professional trainings for groups of therapists seeking to integrate the model into their own practice. I'm consulting with university graduate programs about teaching the model as an established theoretical approach, and I've encouraged further clinical research to study the results of clients who have followed the Awareness Integration journey.

In so many ways, the community of Awareness Integration is expanding. I have invited friends and colleagues to take the same written version of the Awareness Integration journey that you have followed in this book, and the results have been consistently positive. I decided to proceed through all the steps of the model in written form myself, and even after creating this model and utilizing it myself previously, I was struck by the profound new awareness and experiences of healing that emerged for me.

You too are now a vital part of this community, and I invite you to keep your eyes open for ways that you can share your experience with others. Here are a few possibilities for spreading the word about Awareness Integration:

- If you are married, bring your spouse into the picture.
  Earlier we discussed how you can strengthen and enhance your new commitment to your relationship by sharing your own work with Awareness Integration with your partner. We talked about exploring your relationship

143

needs together through creating a shared mission statement, and then establishing mutual goals for you to pursue as a couple. Now you can go further and suggest that your spouse use this book to navigate the Awareness Integration trail step by step on his or her own. I've had the privilege of guiding couples through the model together. It's quite affirming to see the beauty of each person supporting their partner as an individual. When one person is talking and sharing their responses to the questions of the model, the other person is providing a safe and contained space for exploration and growth. Each person feels truly cared for, and the entire process can deepen the bond of the relationship in a very different way. I should point out, however, that this is not something to be undertaken during the throes of significant marital conflict. I trust that you will see a professional marriage and family therapist for that.

- Share your experience in completing the exercises of this book with your therapist, counselor, or coach.

  Tell that person what specifically clicked for you in cultivating valuable awareness and facilitating emotional release. Where and when did you note significant shifts in your thoughts, feelings, and behavior, and how have those shifts translated into tangible change in your life? Perhaps there is something you gained that you can build on with the help of your therapist, or leftover blocks or questions that your therapist can assist you with now.

- Tell your family or friends about what you learned through Awareness Integration.

  When you begin to live by new values and intentions, people around you are quite likely to notice the change. The more aware you are about everything in your life, the more conscious you become in your choices; and the more accountability and responsibility you display toward others around you, the more satisfying and rewarding your life will become. Someone you know may ask, "What have you been doing for yourself?" Then you have the opportunity to authentically share with that person what you have learned through Awareness Integration.

- Start a book club or study group to bring others into the circle of understanding of the Awareness Integration Model.

  You may have several friends or acquaintances wondering what new teachings you may have been introduced to, so launching a group to explore the model together can be a natural extension to simply mentioning this book to individuals. Perhaps group members will choose to commit to following the journey as guided by the book and then get together weekly or monthly to discuss their experiences. The sharing can enrich and deepen the learning for each person, beckoning them to maintain the commitment of visiting the next life areas. As I continue to utilize the model in my work with

individual clients, I also look forward to guiding small groups of people through the Awareness Integration journey together in a shared space. Witnessing one person's experience at any stage of the model can send powerful ripples to others in the group, and the group's empathy and support heightens what happens to anyone who takes time in the spotlight. In a group dynamic, Awareness Integration can truly take on a life of its own.
• Take the Awareness Integration journey again.
You can definitely build on your changes that resulted from completing this book by going back and doing the model again in a year or perhaps two. You will likely find that taking the journey a second or third time will be a richer or deeper experience—and, of course, it will be easier since you are already familiar with the process. As you compare your new experience with what you encountered the first time you tapped into Awareness Integration, you can see and appreciate your own growth. If you have entered any kind of life transition during the period between your journeys, you may have an even wider lens to view the new places you have moved into during that time. When you do take the journey again, remember to revisit your collages to anchor your new values and intentions. Do they need to be updated? It should be fun to spruce them up. Then, once again, you may have others in your life who pick up on your changes and ask you about what's behind it. Hopefully, you will feel eager to assist them in pointing to Awareness Integration as a potential new resource for them.

CONTACT ME

If you have made the choice to get involved with Awareness Integration, I'd love to hear your stories. Whether you are a therapist exploring the model and integrating it in your work with clients, or you are a reader who has followed the Awareness Integration trail through this book, I would greatly appreciate anything you choose to share about your experience.

The more I hear from you, the more I will be able to advance and evolve this new model. Every therapeutic approach is a work in progress, and I am committed to finding ways to make the Awareness Integration Model stronger and more effective as I go along. I certainly welcome your input.

Just as important, it's always gratifying and enriching to learn about what anyone who is devoted to their healing and growth has discovered, and how they have cultivated positive change. We're all in this human community together, and we have so much to offer one another. So feel free to send me an e-mail at any time. And may your own Awareness Integration journey continue to enrich your life in every aspect of it.

Contact the Author

Foojan Zeine, PsyD
5536 Tampa Ave., Tarzana, CA 91356
818-648-2140
Websites: http://www.awarenessintegration.com/ or http://www.foojan.com/
E-mail: Foojan@foojan.com

Appendix A

Emotional-Release Exercise

When you say I am _____ (fill in a negative belief about yourself from this section)

How do you feel? What is the emotion that arises when you say that belief
    to yourself?

Where do you experience this feeling in your body?

On a scale of zero to ten, what is the intensity of that feeling?

Close your eyes. Focus on the area of your body where you experience that
    feeling. Feel the emotion, and allow it to take you with the muscles of your
    body to the first time you ever experienced this feeling and told yourself
    _____ (fill in the blank with the negative belief about yourself).

Write down or speak out loud the first or the earliest memory that appears.

As you see the younger you in the memory, how were you thinking about
    yourself at that time?

Notice if it was a new negative self-belief.

How did the younger you feel about yourself?

Where is this feeling in your body?

What is the intensity from zero to ten?

Allow this feeling with the muscles of your body to take you to the first
time you felt this kind of feeling and told yourself, "I am _____" (fill in the
new negative self-belief). Open your eyes. Write down or speak this memory
and what you found in visiting it. Write or speak your visual, auditory, and
all-felt-sense memory.

Look over what you have uncovered about this memory again. As you focus on this memory, what do you think about the young you in the memory?
How do you feel about the younger you in the memory?

Ask the younger you in the memory what you need. Offer empathy and understanding related to that need. Validate that you as the child did not get what you needed at that time. Remind your child self that as a future version of that child you know you have survived the ordeal and are ready to take care of the child's emotional need, and that you are assessing as a grown-up how to fulfill what is needed now.

On a scale of zero to ten, what is the intensity of the felt feeling?

Now close your eyes and focus on the area of your body where you experi- ence that feeling. Allow this experience in your body to take you again to the first time that you had a similar experience. Write or speak the memory.

What is the intensity of the feeling from zero to ten now?

Breathe deeply. After a few moments, focus on that emotion and say to your- self, "release." Try to bring the intensity of the emotion as low as possible.

Ask yourself, "As I look at myself with (person/people in the area or the category itself, i.e., money, career, etc.), what do I think and feel about myself?" Notice if a different negative core belief comes up. If yes, go through the process again. If neutral or positive beliefs surface, relax your breath and take a moment to simply rest. Then open your eyes.

LAB WORK

Allow yourself to be present with the twelve questions of this area/category as you are living your daily life to gain more real-time awareness. If you no- tice more negative reactions and memories, then continue emotional releasing until you experience neutral/positive thoughts and emotions.

Now answer the following questions related to this area:

- Who do you want/intend to be?
- How do you want to think, feel, and act?
- What specific goals will be helpful in actualizing your intentions?
- What is the concrete action plan that will set you on the right course and keep you on it? Write a timely, tangible, achievable, concrete goal in this area.
- Write specific and timed action plan for each stage of the goal.
- Write your chosen self-identity:
  o Values
  o Emotion
  o Behaviors
  o Create a collage based on your chosen values and goals in this area, and put it in a visible location.
- Live your chosen self.

Appendix B

Step-by-Step Guide to the Awareness Integration Model

Here is a step-by-step guide of the questions in the Awareness Integration Model that can be utilized when exploring every area of life. Address each of these questions for each stop you make on your Awareness Integration journey:

What do you think of _____ (person/people in the area or the category, i.e., money, career, etc.)? Write both positive and negative thoughts.

How do you feel about _____ (person/people in the area or the category, i.e., money, career, etc.)? Write both positive/pleasurable and negative/uncomfortable emotions.

How do you behave toward _____ (person/people in the area or the category, i.e., money, career, etc.)? Write both actions/behaviors that have created favorable results and ones that have created unfavorable results.

How does the way you think, feel, and behave toward _____ (person/people in the area or the category, i.e., money, career, etc.) impact your life and others' lives? Write the positive and negative impacts.

When _____ (person/people in the area) are around you, what do you assume they think about you? When others are around you in the area of _____ (category, i.e., money, sex, etc.), what do you assume they think about you? Write your positive and negative assumptions.

When _____ (person/people in the area) are around you, how do you assume they feel about you? When others are around you in the area of _____ (category, i.e., money, sex, etc.), what do you assume they feel about you? Write your positive and negative assumptions.

When _____ (person/people in the area) are around you, how do you experience his/her/their behavior toward you?

How has the way that you assume _____ (person/people in the area)
   think, feel, and behave toward you when they are around you impacted
   your life and others' lives? Write the positive and negative impact.
When you are present with _____ (person/people in the area/category),
   what do you think about yourself? Write positive and negative thoughts.
When you are present with _____ (person/people in the area/category),
   how do you feel about yourself? Write positive and negative emotions.
When you are present with _____ (person/people in the area/category),
   how do you behave toward yourself? Write positive and negative behaviors.
How does the way that you think, feel, and behave toward yourself around
   _____ (person/people in the area/category) impact your life and others' lives? Write the positive and negative impact.

Appendix C

An Example of the
Awareness Integration Journey

Throughout the book you have read many real-life examples of women and men of all ages and backgrounds who have made important life changes by following the Awareness Integration journey. Most of those illustrations emerged from one-on-one work with a therapist leading the client through the model in person. Below is an example of one of my clients who completed all the steps of the model the same way you are approaching Awareness Integration: by reading the questions in this book and writing her answers down in her journal.

The selected excerpts from her complete responses are not meant to show any one "correct" way to utilize the journey mapped out in this book. However, you may find her process helpful as you explore the most effective and productive way for you to facilitate your own experience with Awareness Integration.

PEOPLE

I think people are unique and diverse, very complex. It appears that the duality of these constantly meaning-producing creatures continues. It never ceases to amaze me how people perceive, react, and act. I think that every single human being lives in their own bubble and can only see the world through that bubble. They can be loving and hateful. The same person is capable of loving and hatred and brutality. Very selfish while self-giving. How does that choice come about?

Women are caring, powerful, and manipulative. Men are calculative, child-like, pleasure-oriented, power-seeking individuals. Both genders are very similar in their needs for closeness and love. Men have a relationship with sexuality that is very different than women.

I feel connected with the human race, and yet not with people I don't know. I feel generally safe unless I pick up a disturbing and unfriendly vibe from people. I yearn to connect with kind people and lose a sense of belonging to the species when I sense brutality. When I am alone, I feel disconnected, as if I am only an observer. When I see kindness, I feel safe and joy. When I see coldness and anger, I feel threatened and want to run away. If I believe that humans are brutal and vicious, then I prefer not to exist. I don't like the feeling of vigilance and needing to be on my toes for survival constantly.

I am cordial, kind, and respectful to people in general. I do judge in my mind and categorize and then accept all aspects of my own categorization in my head. I love people, watching and guessing what they are like and what they are thinking. Their variety amazes me. There is a beauty in people who are happy, playful, and caring, and I love being around them.

The impact of my way of thinking, feeling, and behavior has kept me safe and successful in my life. I moved to the U.S. as a teenager and have been living, surviving, and moving forward on my own, with minimum harm from people. People have been there for me and have helped me move forward and onto a higher ground. I feel grateful toward all the people who have facilitated growth and greatness around me.

I assume that people think of me as beautiful, exotic, powerful, and snobbish. Ha ha. I assume that people feel safe with me . . . very neutral.

They behave very cordially and courteously.

The impact has been that I feel safe wherever I go and am open to meeting people from all over the world.

I think of myself as powerful and presentable beside people. I feel proud and am more observant of them and what their needs and personality is. I am nice to myself and supportive and at times protective. At times, with some people, I feel scared and more protective, and think that they have a negative agenda, they want to manipulate me to use me somehow, or that they are lying to me to get something from me. They don't see me or care for me; I am just an object to be used.

The impact is that I have been able to become at ease and effective speaking in front of groups of people.

When I think, "I've been used," I feel disgusted and sad, in my gut and chest, 8 in intensity.

As I feel the disgust and sadness, and allowing these feelings in my gut and chest to take me to the first or earliest time that I said to myself "I've been used," I have the experience of two memories both around three years old. One was with my uncle who had created a model for literacy and was teaching the alphabet in a rhythmic way. He had taught me that way and wanted to show the effectiveness of the model in front of a large audience that included people in the educational system and the government. When I went on stage, I froze and could not read. He was very angry at me, and my mother was very angry at me since that day was a waste and a humiliation for them. I felt sad and broken, guilty at first and angry for him putting me in this position and then yelling at me when I got scared. I felt lonely with no one protecting me and setting me up to fail. As if I was used for their advantage rather than taking care of me. I felt sad and powerless. As I look at the 3-year-old little girl, she thought she was bad, useless, can't do anything right, ruined it for others, responsible for the damage, angry at being put in that position, sad for not having anyone on her side. She needed her mom and uncle to soothe her, calm her down and tell her that she was just scared and not prepped since this was the first time she had to face so many people and instantaneously become a public speaker.

As I imagined hugging the 3-year-old and holding her and telling her in her ears that she did the best that she could do in that instant, and that I was sorry that others had put her in that position, that I was with her and will protect her, I cried, and my sadness released to the intensity of 2.

The other memory was that I was 3 years old and spending time with a family who had four kids. This was a stay-over event. All the kids slept on the floor beside each other. After the first night, I woke up the next morning lower than every other kid on the floor, with my panties down and a feeling of wetness. I was scared and could not figure out what had happened. Why was I like this? What happened? On the second night, after all the kids had gone to sleep, I felt two hands on my ankles pulling me down and bringing my panties down, putting something between my legs and rubbing, and then I felt wet. I was scared, [and] pretended to be [a]sleep. I did not know what was going on, just knew it was not good and was being hidden. I felt shame and disgust by the wetness. As the father of the kids left, I waited until I could not hear him and then pulled my panties up and pulled myself back to my original place of sleep. The next morning everyone was acting the same as before. I was the only one who was confused and ashamed. I called my mom to take me home. When she came to pick me up, they were all so nice to each other that I was confused. What happened those two nights? I could not tell my mom since I did not know what happened and how to describe it. I just felt disgusted in my body and knew that I had been used.

As I look at the 3-year-old in their home, I see that she thought she was different, did not belong to that group; something had happened that should not have but she did not know what. She wanted someone to explain it to her, she wanted to figure all of this out, she needed guidance, protection, and some explanation of why a house that seemed safe and happy turned out to be disgusting all in the dark, and then everyone pretending that all was great when in daylight. How could she ever be safe, how could she assess? Why didn't her mother or father know what happened in that house? How could they miss it? And if they missed it, then how could she find out and keep herself safe?

I held her in my arms and told her that she did not do anything wrong and that I was here to assess and protect her now. She did not have the skills to assess or protect herself at that time, and I was sorry that she was put in that situation at age 3. I told her that I was proud of her and her strength to have pulled through this experience and have survived it well.

My sadness is 2, disgust is 4 in intensity.

FATHER

I think he was a fun guy, a sweet man, a funny man; a great man who did not know how to be a father or a husband. People who know him say that he was a genius at his work and yet they also say with a grin how much of a womanizer he was. His motto was "change three things every two years: car, career, and women," and he did. All I remember from him was that he put my mom [through] a lot of pain due to his flirting and affairs. He was innovative and brought so many new ideas to his businesses and yet was not able to manage and grow the businesses to a large extent. He bankrupted himself before death.

I feel disconnected to him, at times rage for not being my father and not taking care of me. I felt unloved and uncared for. Even when he supposedly came to see me, it was more for the sake of my mother and trying to win her back rather than wanting to spend time with me.

I wanted to see him more often, and he was not around. I acted very quietly and flexible around him when he was around me. After awhile, I gave up and just resented him. I tried not to see him again.

The impact has been that I see men in general in the same realm. I assume they will cheat and only take care of their need. This generalization has created high levels of anxiety in my intimate relationships.

I assume that he thought of me as an obligation to handle. When I was 18 and was an international student who could not continue college due to high tuition fees, which I had to pay myself, he called once after two years and angrily stated that he was very disappointed that I was not going to college while my cousins were all going to medical school. I was shocked. How dare he demand when he never gave?

I assume that he loved me as much as he was capable of loving a child.

He came to see me once every month when I was little. Then he moved to another city and had excuses not to see me.

The impact of the way I assumed he thought and felt about me is that he left me in a standoffish position with my mom. This way I could not even grasp any of his love.

When I was a child I thought of myself beside him as unwanted. As a grown-up I see myself separate and not belonging. I feel sadness and a yearning for him to want me. I also feel compassion for myself for not having a father. I isolate myself and withdraw.

When I say I am unwanted, I feel shame, in my gut, an intensity of 8.

As I allow shame with the muscles of my gut to take me to my first memory when I felt this kind of shame and told myself that I was unwanted, I see myself when I was 7 years old and having to go visit him. His driver took me to his office, and when I went up, he was in a meeting. When his meeting was done he came out and saw me, but did not acknowledge me. Other people in his office were very friendly to me. I waited and waited in his office until it was time for him to finish work so we could go. He told his secretary to take me to the car. When he came down to the car, he was flirting with the secretary outside the car while I was sitting in the car. Then he took me to a restaurant with music, and all of his friends. He was laughing, and drinking and dining with all of them. I felt weird, not belonging in this scene. I knew my mom would be upset when she found out later. I could not get his attention for more than couple of seconds at a time, and it was mostly to quiet me down. I felt like an outsider and did not know what to do except to sit quietly and observe his and others' behavior. I felt shame being there, witnessing grown-ups flirting in a sexual way in a nightclub restaurant scene. I felt shame because I thought that I was a burden, an obligation to be handled, and not a person whom my father had the desire to spend time with.

Now I am sad with the grief of not ever having a father who was there for me. Even when I got to be there with him, he did not want to spend time with me or get to know me. He obviously was interested in other people and had fun with others, but not me. He just wanted to ignore me, or get over the time of his visitations, or get rid of me. I no longer wanted to go for visitations.

I also remember when I went to his new home with his new wife. They had a little son together. His new wife was very nice to me; I got lots of attention. But I did not like it that there was another child that was replacing me for him. Worse, this child got to live with him and I didn't. I guess he did not want me bad enough to have me stay. He looked at my mom with sad eyes, not wanting to let her go, and yet not being able to control himself with his cheating. So my mom finally got fed up and called it quits.

Wow . . . I just realized how I create this pattern with my sensitivities and leave relationships due to intolerance of any types of flirtation, and yet men get shocked and insist that I come back with their sad eyes.

The shame is 2 in intensity, the sadness 4.

The little girl wanted to be seen, heard, cared for, valued, played with, and paid attention to. She deserved to have all of that as a normal child. I hugged her and told her that I am sorry that her father was not capable of giving her all of that, but that did not mean that she was unwanted. It just meant that he did not know how to pay attention to kids. He was much more pleasure oriented than love oriented, or being able to attend to his commitments. I told her that I was here and promised her to see her, hear her, value her, and take care of her from here on.

Shame 0, sadness 1, grief 2, yearning 0.

Now that I look at myself beside my father, I think I was lucky to have his creativity and mental genius and unlucky to have him as a father who did not have the skills of fatherhood. Oh well, with these cards that were dealt for my life, I turned out pretty OK.

MOTHER

I think she is a very loving and forgiving person. She has a childlike purity that is joyous; this also has caused her to be abused emotionally and financially by many people in her surroundings. She was always ahead of her time. She used to be very accepting and forgiving of all that has happened to her, but now she is very judgmental and yet forgiving. I think she has become more judgmental because of her many years of marriage to a man who lies and judges everyone; it is bound to rub off. She is a great human being that is loved by everyone, yet not good in the mother role. Her career and relationships always took a priority over her role in the responsibility of being a mother and fulfilling my needs. She was a great mentor and inspirational pusher toward excellence, but not in a mothering role.

I feel love for her; she and all of her accomplishments impress me. I feel sad for her with all that she went through in her life. I feel disconnected to her. I feel angry at her for not being the mother that I needed. I feel shame about some of her decision making in life. I feel abandoned and rejected by her for her inability to be close to me. I feel unwanted by her.

I have acted in a superficial way toward her all these years. I see her or call her out of obligation. For the past 40 years, I have only seen her five times, for a period of one week each visit.

The impact is that I have kept myself away from her. I became very independent very early in life. I have learned and held her value system, her purity and loving essence, and have been living on my own.

I assume that she thinks that I have potential but that I have not achieved all that she expected me to achieve. She is proud to hear from others how successful I am, but it is never enough. In her eyes, I have to always achieve more.

I assume she feels guilt toward me and resentful toward me for feeling guilty.

She acts verbally loving and yet very judgmental. She will always tell me what I have done wrong and what else I should be doing. Her way of supporting me is to tell me my shortcomings and how I should be while she superficially expresses loving terms of endearments.

The impact of my assumption about her on my life has been devastating. I have felt unwanted, a burden, never good enough, and that I don't belong to anyone or anywhere. That has impacted all of my deep, close, and intimate relationships. Ultimately, I carry the notion that I have no value for people; if I did not have enough value for my mother then I certainly have no value for others.

I think of myself beside her as a stranger, a balloon with a string that is not attached anywhere, not landing, not staying, not easy in my skin, never good enough nor accepted. I feel sadness and shame. I observe myself and tell myself that I have to want her, I have to love her, I have to be courteous. I feel a sense of guilt for not feeling connected to her. The impact is that I feel incomplete and forced. I tend to run constantly after the next and the next . . . not being fulfilled with what is . . . to always excel to prove to her that I am finally good.

When I tell myself that I don't have value, I feel sad and powerless, in my gut and back shoulders, intensity of 9.

As I trace my emotions of sadness and powerlessness in my gut and shoulder to the first time or earliest time that I said to myself I have no value, it is when I was 6 years old and was sitting on the stairs outside our home with two of my cousins since my mother was not home yet. She was rarely home, and even when she was, she was tired or sleepy and needed a massage from me rather than nurturing me. She demanded service versus giving service to me. It appeared to me that her work and her friends were more valuable than my needs and me.

As I looked at the 6-year-old, I saw that she needed to be cared for, pampered, and be made a priority. She needed to know and see the evidence and feel that she was valuable enough for Mom to make me a priority.

I held the 6-year-old in my arms and told her that she has value for me and that she is a priority for me and many other people around her. I also promised to take her away from all the places that she felt devalued and to make sure that people would see her value.

Feelings changed to sadness 2, powerlessness 0.

Now when I look at my mom I think that she only knew that way of being a mother. Yes, she was dedicated to her career, and as a single mother, she needed to do that. She thought others were taking care of me, and since she loved attention from others, she thought I was OK being with others.

I feel neutral at this time. I feel valuable as a person.

LOOKING AT MYSELF IN THE MIRROR

I look at me . . . I never thought that I was pretty. Everyone else told me that I was, and yet I always found fault with some part of my body. I still do, now I am saggy due to aging. I get lots of attention for my looks from guys in an admiration/sexual desire way and from women from admiration, envy, and jealousy. Most times this is very uncomfortable. It is as if I am trying to be responsible for their feelings and thoughts. I am tired of that. I like the attention as long as there is no conflict. Yet, at times it creates unwanted attention and friction between someone's desire and my rejection, or a man's desire and his woman's jealousy and rage. Then I feel responsible for the destruction and the friction. I also notice that I gain weight to minimize and distract attention, especially when I am dating, and this upsets my dates. Since I feel responsible, I gain weight to minimize the attention in order to minimize friction. Obviously this does not work for me and my health, since I gain and lose more than 30 pounds every couple of years. The duality of internally thinking that I am ugly, the extra attention and the feedback that I was pretty, and the unwanted attention from people who would create more of a problem all makes for a mess. Today I no longer think that I am ugly. I finally accepted that I am attractive, but now I want to keep it and am defying the aging process. This saga never ends, just shifts elements.

When I look into my eyes, I think I am a decent, loving, intelligent, committed person. I also feel tired. I have emotionally struggled all my life and have had to learn life as I had to survive it, as a child in between two parents who were more interested in themselves, and I had to immigrate on my own and build a life on my own. That has been a rough road.

I feel exhausted at times, with sadness and a grief for a normal childhood and all that came with it. I feel shame for decisions that I have made with all good intentions and based on my noble values but that did not fit the norm of the cultures that I lived in. I am angry to have to answer to people who judge me for my decisions, while I go through the shame of being judged.

I have been much more nurturing toward myself in recent years. I used to isolate myself due to shame and humiliation. I used to attempt to please others who were nasty or abusive toward me, just to be liked by everyone and forgive me for the perfect human being that I am not. I used to need to excel in every aspect of my life to prove to everyone that I was worthy of their attention and love. That left me sad and empty inside. I did not feel that I belonged to anyone: any family, any city, or any culture.

As I feel the sadness in my heart, the thought of "I am alone" pops up. When I say I am alone, my heart begins to ache, and my chest feels painful, with the intensity of 7. I stay with the pain and go with the muscles of my heart to the first time I felt this kind of sadness and said to myself, "I am alone." The memory is of being less than one year old and only able to crawl. I was feeling sad, sitting in a corner crying. There were many people in the room, but I wanted my mom. She was not there. I felt powerless and sad, as if no one could give me what I wanted and it was just the way it was. The little girl wanted her mom, and to feel that she belonged to the one that was hers, and not all these other people whom she did not belong to. After allowing her to feel her sadness and release it, the intensity drops to 3. I told her that I am here and she belongs to me and will always belong to me regardless of how many people are around. The intensity number lowered to neutral.

As I look at myself in the mirror, I see a smile. I have come a long way through all the ups and downs of life. I have made it. I have arrived, regardless of the circumstances and the obstacles. I feel powerful.

THE RETURN JOURNEY OF AWARENESS INTEGRATION

God

I intend to be the essence of love and acceptance.
I think of how we all have the essence and are able to tap into it. I feel blessed, grand, humble, gratitude.
I act in a loving, respectful, and accepting way toward myself and others.

Universe

I intend to be the essence of creativity.
I think that I am part of a bigger picture and a process. Life is an experience.
    I feel joy and intrigued by living my experience.
I act according to my principles toward the betterment of all.

Nature

I intend to be responsible and grateful.
I think that I belong as a species on this earth and have a responsibility to
  share the space with other species.
I feel a sense of belonging and joy.
I act toward the preservation and creation with respect to all.

Myself

I intend to be Loving, Accepting, Productive, Healthy, and Responsible.
I think I have been blessed with an intelligence that I intend to utilize in a way
  that impacts people in a positive way.
I feel love and joy, warmth in my heart, and filled with gratitude. I act on
  behalf of my physical and mental health.

Action Plan

I will exercise six days a week (two days of walking for an hour and a half;
  two days with a trainer for 1.2 hours; two days on the trampoline for 30
  minutes).
I will bring my weight to 150 pounds and maintain it.
I will eat vegetables, fish and 10 percent meat, no sugar and carbs. I will
  meditate for 10 minutes daily.
I will replace negative thoughts about myself with positive and realistic
  thoughts as I become aware of them.

Love

I intend to cherish, give, and receive Love.
I think that Love is the essence of our being and the doorway to joy. I feel
  warmth and safety with Love.
I act lovingly toward myself and others.

Action Plan

Meditate 10 minutes per day and experience love.
Write in my Gratitude journal every night five things that created love during
  the day.
Even when angry and frustrated about something or when I judge someone,
  or feel judged by someone, I will seek to find a loving thought to replace
  it and create a loving action toward myself or others.

Mother

I intend to be loving and accepting toward her.

I think that she has given me life, strength, open-mindedness, a sense of discovery, the need to grow and excel, amazing loving principles, and beauty.

I feel forgiving and clear about all that was expected which I did not get, and blessed for me life and all that I got.

I act with caring and respect.

Action Plan

Call biweekly.
Meet with her once a year.

Godmother

I intend to be loving and accepting.

I think that I learned unconditional love from her and I am most grateful for all of who she is and has given me.

I feel love, gratitude, and bliss. I act lovingly.

Action Plan

Call biweekly.
Visit her once a year.

My Mate

I intend to be loving, accepting, passionate, dedicated, respectful, accountable, and the creator of fun, joy, and play.

I think that he has given me the gift of the best relationship of my life, and that I deserve it. I am committed to creating a joyous, passionate, loving, and committed relationship.

I feel blessed, loved, loving, joyous.

I act in a way to express all that I think and feel for him and this relationship.

Action Plan

Express my joy, love, and gratitude. Spend quality time together.

Create fun and games to play.

Meet his family and introduce him to my family. Take four trips per year together.

Shift my untrusting thoughts to trusting him, and to reality-based thinking.

Money

I intend to be prosperous, generous, responsible, and accountable. I feel grateful to have the ability to create money.
I act responsibly and plan for the future.

Action Plan

Save $100 a day to be put in my savings account. Invest in retirement accounts.
Buy only what I need, and once a month buy one item out of desire and not need.
Sell or purge items that I don't use.

Career

I intend to be successful and fulfilled.
I think that I am in a field of inspiring people. That is a blessing.
I feel fulfilled with my work and my creativity and reinvention of my work.
  I act responsibly and accountable toward my field and all.

Action Plan

Complete my current research project within six months.
Create an academic course as another avenue to present my work. Write weekly blogs for my website.
Follow up on my new, creative idea with the goal of bringing it to fruition as a book or a stage play . . . or both!

Friends

I intend to love and cherish all my friends.
I think that my friends are my true source and resource.
I feel blessed with all the great love and wisdom around me.
I act lovingly and respectfully.

Action Plan

Continue weekly socialization with various friends.

My Anchoring Process

Values: Love, commitment, being responsible and accountable, dedication, prosperous, generous, and acceptance.

Emotions: Love, passion, joy, happiness, blessed, gratitude, calmness, and fulfilled.

Behaviors: Loving, caring, responsibly, committed, accountable, with generosity.

Notes

CHAPTER ONE

1. Nathaniel Branden, *The Art of Living Consciously: The Power of Awareness to Transform Everyday Life* (New York: Simon & Schuster, 1997), 10.
2. Michio Kaku, *The Future of the Mind: The Scientific Quest to Understand, Enhance, and Empower the Mind* (New York: Doubleday, 2014), 57.
3. Daniel J. Siegel, *The Developing Mind: How Relationships and the Brain Interact to Shape Who We Are* (New York: Guilford, 1999).
4. Henry P. Stapp, *Mindful Universe: Quantum Mechanics and the Participating Observer* (Berlin: Springer, 2007).

CHAPTER SIX

1. Allan N. Schore, *Affect Regulation and the Repair of the Self* (New York: Norton, 2003).

Bibliography

Beck, Aaron T. *Cognitive Therapy of Depression*. New York: Guilford, 1979.
———. *Depression: Causes and Treatment*. Philadelphia: University of Pennsylvania Press, 1972.
Bendersky, Margaret, and Michael Lewis. "Environmental Risks, Biological Risks, and Developmental Outcome." *Developmental Psychology* 30, no. 4 (July 1994): 484–94.
Branden, Nathaniel. *The Art of Living Consciously: The Power of Awareness to Transform Everyday Life*. New York: Simon & Schuster, 1997.
Coe, Christopher L., Gabriele R. Lubach, Mary L. Schneider, Donald J. Dierschke, and William B. Ershler. "Early Rearing Conditions Alter Immune Responses in the Developing Infant Primate." *Pediatrics* 90, no. 3 (September 1992): 505–9.
Earleywine, Mitchell. *Mind-Altering Drugs: The Science of Subjective Experience*. Oxford: Oxford University Press, 2005.
Ellis, Albert, and Debbie Joffe-Ellis. *Rational Emotive Behavior Therapy: Theories of Psychotherapy*. Washington, DC: American Psychological Association, 2011.
Kaku, Michio. *The Future of the Mind: The Scientific Quest to Understand, Enhance, and Empower the Mind*. New York: Doubleday, 2014.
Levine, Peter A. *Healing Trauma: A Pioneering Program for Restoring the Wisdom of Your Body*. Boulder, CO: Sounds True, 2008.
Pinker, Steven. *How the Mind Works*. New York: Norton, 1997.
Rossi, Ernest Lawrence, and David B. Cheek. *Mind-Body Therapy: Ideodynamic Healing in Hypnosis*. New York: Norton, 1988.
Salkovskis, Paul M. *Frontiers of Cognitive Therapy*. New York: Guilford, 1996.
Schore, Allan N. *Affect Regulation and the Repair of the Self*. New York: Norton, 2003.
Shapiro, Francine. *Eye Movement Desensitization and Reprocessing: Basic Principles, Protocols, and Procedures*. New York: Guilford, 1995.
Siegel, Daniel J. *The Developing Mind: How Relationships and the Brain Interact to Shape Who We Are*. New York: Guilford, 1999.

Stapp, Henry P. *Mindful Universe: Quantum Mechanics and the Participating Observer.* Berlin: Springer, 2007.

Teasdale, John D. "Emotion and Two Kinds of Meaning: Cognitive Therapy and Applied Cognitive Science." *Behaviour Research and Therapy* 31, no. 4 (1993): 339–54.

Index

abuse: by father, 78, 80, 110; traumas and, 44
achievement, 49, 125, 142
addiction: illness, disabilities and, 94–99; recovery and, 127
advice, 34, 70
affairs, 65
Affect Regulation and the Repair of the Self (Schore), 81
aggression, 15
alignment, xi, 141; behavior in, 140; choices and, 137; with desires, 5; silence and, 132
anger, 47, 153; aggression and, 15; with God, 109
anxiety, 154; avoidance of, 54; beliefs and, 38; grief and, 24; as natural response, 81; symptoms of, xiii
association: of emotions, 116; feelings and, 37; God, trauma and, 110; with memories, 13, 120
assumptions, 66, 150; about addiction, 99; about caretaker, 89; by children, 74; about father, 79; about feelings, 19, 57, 70, 74, 89; about God, 112; impacts of, 157; by in-laws, 53; about judgment, 18; about mother, 83; partners and, 58, 62, 64; by people, 34, 40, 97; as positive and

negative, 45, 74; about sex, 70; by siblings, 46; by significant person, 49; about thoughts, 57
atheism, 109, 111, 113
attitude, 118; of acceptance, 127; anchoring of, 136–39; as different, 113; as evolved, 39; exploration of, 30; goals and, 16; identification of, 35; impact of, 18; about money, 38; observations about, 33; as positive, 3; as receptive, 71; toward sex, 68; values and, 139; toward work, 29
authority, 32
Awareness Integration Model, xiii; clients and, 3, 37, 118; contact regarding, 145–46; development of, 5; example of, 151–63; guide to, 149–50; as journey, 9, 33, 95, 117–42, 143–45; mastery and, 1; preparation for, 10–11; working with, 12, 43, 106

behavior, 137, 149; toward affair, 66; as affirming, 129; in alignment, 140; toward career, 33; toward caretaker, 89; as changed, 132; toward children, 74; as critical, 141; toward death, 115; toward father, 79; of friends, 20; toward God, 111; toward illness,

About the Author

Foojan Zeine, PsyD, is an international speaker, author, psychotherapist, and life and executive coach. She is the originator and the author of the Awareness Integration psychotherapeutic model. Zeine is the founder, CEO, and the clinical director for the Personal Growth Institute, a not-for-profit organization that offers psychotherapy services to the multicultural and multilingual population. She speaks at many academic and nonacademic institutions, including the University of California, Los Angeles; the University of Southern California; the University of California, Santa Barbara; California State University, Long Beach; the Massachusetts Institute of Technology; and Harvard University. She was an invited guest on the Dr. Phil show, FOX, Voice of America, GEM TV, KIRN 670AM. She also hosts an Internet television shows "Inner Voice" www.foojan.com